The Neck and the Sword

Other titles in the Palestine Pamphlets series

The Destruction of Palestine Is the Destruction of the Earth

by Andreas Malm

Moral Abdication: How the World Failed to Stop the Destruction of Gaza

by Didier Fassin

Resisting Erasure: Capital, Imperialism and Race in Palestine

by Adam Hanieh, Robert Knox, and Rafeef Ziadah

The Neck and the Sword

Palestine's Unfinished Struggle

Rashid Khalidi
Tariq Ali

VERSO
London • New York

First published by Verso 2026

Chapter 1 appeared in an earlier form as "The Neck and the Sword" in *New Left Review* 147 (May/June 2024)

The manufacturer's authorized representative in the EU for product safety (GPSR) is LOGOS EUROPE, 9 rue Nicolas Poussin, 17000, La Rochelle, France
contact@logoseurope.eu

1 3 5 7 9 10 8 6 4 2

Verso
UK: 6 Meard Street, London W1F 0EG
US: 207 East 32nd Street, New York, NY 10016
versobooks.com

Verso is the imprint of New Left Books

ISBN-13: 978-1-83674-576-1
ISBN-13: 978-1-83674-578-5 (US EBK)
ISBN-13: 978-1-83674-577-8 (UK EBK)

British Library Cataloguing in Publication Data
A catalogue record for this book is available from the British Library

Library of Congress Cataloging-in-Publication Data
A catalog record for this book is available
from the Library of Congress
Library of Congress Control Number: 2026945547

Typeset in Sabon MT by Hewer Text UK Ltd, Edinburgh
Printed and bound by CPI Group (UK) Ltd, Croydon, CR0 4YY

In memory of all the Palestinians
who have suffered and died from 1917 onward

Contents

Publisher's Note

The three discussions below took place over two years between 2024 and 2026. The first was published as an interview for *New Left Review*'s May/June 2024 issue. Over sixty years, *NLR* has integrated the interview as a crucial part of its repertoire and raised it to the level of an art form. The second conversation was a joint initiative between Tariq Ali and Rashid Khalidi to bring their analyses more firmly into the present, even as constant political developments make such an endeavor somewhat Sisyphean. The third interview was unplanned but necessitated by the commencement of the US–Israeli war against Iran.

The Neck and the Sword is the latest in Verso's Palestine Pamphlet series, a project launched in the midst of Israel's genocide in Gaza to provide sharp, urgent political analysis of the evolving situation in Palestine. Other books in the series include Andreas Malm's *The Destruction of Palestine Is the Destruction of the Earth*, Didier Fassin's *Moral Abdication: How the World Failed to Stop the Destruction of Gaza*, and

Resisting Erasure: Capital, Imperialism and Race in Palestine from Adam Hanieh, Robert Knox and Rafeef Ziadah.

Rashid Khalidi and Tariq Ali bring a lifetime of learning and experience to this three-part conversation about Palestine's history, present, and future. Rashid Khalidi is an esteemed scholar of Palestinian history and author of *The Hundred Years' War on Palestine: A History of Settler Colonialism and Resistance, 1917–2017*, an unmatched work of scholarship that has been translated into dozens of languages and educated a new generation of supporters in Palestine's struggle for liberation. Tariq Ali is a writer and historian who has been active in the Palestine solidarity movement since he first visited the country in the 1960s.

1.

May 10, 2024

Tariq Ali: Let's start with the present, not just in the sense of the horrors being inflicted on Palestine right now, but the present as part of Palestine's still-active past. The brutal Anglo-Zionist repression of the great Arab Revolt of 1936–39 was followed by the Nakba of 1948, the Six-Day War in 1967, the 1982 siege of Beirut led by Ariel Sharon, and the massacres of Sabra and Shatila, the two Intifadas, the continuous raining down of terror by Israel since then. Yet the post–October 7 genocide seems to have had a bigger global impact than any of these.

Rashid Khalidi: Yes, something has shifted globally. I'm not sure why those historic episodes did not have the effect of completely changing the narrative—the popular narrative, in particular.

I don't want to speculate about things like social media. But this has been the first genocide that a generation has witnessed in real time, on their own devices. Was it the first atrocity in recent times in which the US, Britain, and the other Western powers were direct participants, unlike others, in Sudan or Myanmar? Did the work of pro-Palestinian advocates over a generation or more prepare people for this? I don't know. But you are right that as a result of the horrors that have been inflicted on Gaza over seven continuous months, and which are still being inflicted now, something new has happened. The displacement of three-quarters of a million people in 1948 did not produce the same impact. The 1936–39 Arab Revolt is almost completely forgotten. None of those earlier events had anything like this effect.

TA: The Arab Revolt has always fascinated me as one of the major episodes of anticolonial struggle, and one which has had far less attention than it deserves. It began as a strike, became a series of strikes, then developed into a huge national uprising which had British forces tied down for over three years. Could you give us an explanation of its origins, development, and consequences?

RK: The Arab Revolt was essentially a popular uprising, one on a massive scale. The traditional Palestinian leadership was taken by surprise, just as Arafat and the PLO leadership were surprised by the First Intifada in 1987. Both uprisings were sparked by minor incidents. In the case of the Arab Revolt, it was the death in battle of Shaikh Izz ad-Din al-Qassam in November 1935, killed by British forces. Born in 1882 in Jableh, on the Syrian coast, al-Qassam was a religious scholar trained at Al-Azhar, and a militant anti-imperialist who fought against all the Western powers in the region, beginning with the Italians in Libya in 1911, then the French Mandate forces in Syria in 1919–20. He ended up in British Mandate Palestine, where he lived and worked mainly among the peasantry and the urban poor. Al-Qassam's killing had an enormous amplitude, such that within a few months it had helped to detonate the longest general strike in interwar colonial history. The best account is by Ghassan Kanafani, the great Palestinian writer assassinated by the Israelis in 1972; it was to have been the first chapter of his history of the Palestinian struggle, unfinished at his death.[1]

Kanafani's analysis stands to this day. Among other things, he underlined the economic impact on the popular classes of increased Jewish migration to Palestine in the 1930s, after Hitler came to power; the sacking of Arab workers from factories and construction sites, in line with Ben-Gurion's policy of "Jewish Labour Only"; the eviction of 20,000 peasant families from their fields and orchards, sold to Zionist settlers by absentee landlords; and rising poverty. These popular revolts erupt when people reach a point where they just cannot go on as before, and in this case social anger combined with powerful national and religious feelings. The Palestinians rose up against the full might of the British Empire—which, in a century and a half, had not been forced to grant independence to a single colonial dependency, with the sole exception of Ireland in 1921. The Arab

Revolt was crushed by what was still the world's most powerful empire, but the Palestinians fought for over three years, with perhaps a sixth of the adult male population killed, injured, in prison, or in exile. In the annals of the interwar period, this was an unprecedented attempt to overthrow colonial rule. It was only suppressed by the deployment of 100,000 troops and the RAF. This is a forgotten page in Palestinian history.

TA: Did not this defeat also lead to a demoralization among the Palestinian masses, so that when the Nakba proper began in 1947, they still had not recovered from the terror of 1936–39?

RK: The defeat of the Arab Revolt created a heavy legacy that affected the Palestinian people for decades. As Kanafani wrote, the Nakba, "the second chapter of the Palestinian defeat"—from the end of 1947 to the middle of 1948—was amazingly short, because it was only the conclusion of this long and bloody chapter, which had lasted from April 1936 to September 1939.[2] What the British did was later copied in almost every detail by the Zionist leaders from Ben-Gurion onward. For that reason alone, it's worth recalling the cost to Palestinian society. At least 2,000 homes were blown up, crops destroyed, over a hundred rebels executed for possessing firearms. All this was accompanied by curfews, detention without trial, internal exile, torture, practices like tying villagers to the front of steam engines, as a shield against attacks by freedom fighters.

In an Arab population of about a million, 5,000 were killed, 10,000-plus wounded, and over 5,000 political prisoners were left rotting in colonial jails.

TA: In the process of crushing the Arab Revolt, the British gave the Zionist forces that were working with them valuable training in counterinsurgency.

RK: Yes. The Zionists were taught every underhanded colonial technique by counterinsurgency experts like Orde Wingate and other specialists in torture and murder. The British imported veterans from India, like Charles Tegart, the notorious chief of police in Calcutta, the subject of six assassination attempts by Indian nationalists. Some of the same forts and prison camps built by Tegart are still in use by Israel today. They brought in people from Ireland and other places in the empire, like Sudan, where Wingate had started, and where his father's cousin, Reginald Wingate, had been governor-general and an intelligence officer before that.

TA: Orde Wingate, a long-forgotten name. I doubt many readers would even have heard of this demented figure, of whom Montgomery said the best thing he ever did was to be in the plane crash that killed him in Burma in 1944. Who was he and did he have any special links to the Zionist forces? I vaguely recall a BBC TV series on him in 1976 where he was portrayed as a hero.

RK: He was a cold-blooded colonial killer, one who ended up a major general, and who was loathed by many on his own side, as Montgomery's remark suggests; Montgomery also described Wingate as "mentally unbalanced." Churchill, no slouch when it came to inflicting suffering on subject populations, called Wingate "too mad for command." He was born in British India into a pious Plymouth Brethren family. A Christian fundamentalist and a Bible literalist, he promoted the Old Testament version of Jewish redemption. He arrived in Palestine as a captain in military intelligence just as the 1936 uprising was beginning. He knew Arabic, learned Hebrew, and became a key figure in training Haganah and Palmach fighters as "special night squads"—in other words, death squads—to target and kill Palestinian villagers in the mountains, just as the Israeli military and settlers do today. His notoriety was such that on the outbreak of the European war in 1939, the Arab notables demanded that Wingate be expelled from the region. He was. His passport was stamped, prohibiting his return. His job was done. He had trained many of the men who became commanders of the Palmach and later became generals in the Israeli military, like Moshe Dayan and Yigal Allon. Several sites in Israel bear his name, and he is rightly considered the founder of Israeli military doctrine.

TA: He taught them well.

RK: Yes. What was once a British colonial specialty became an Israeli colonial specialty. Everything the Israelis have done they learned from the British—including the laws, the 1945 Defence Emergency Regulations, for example, that the British used against the Irgun. The same laws are still in force, now used against Palestinians. It all comes from the British colonial playbook.

TA: A victory—or even a draw—for the Arab Revolt would have laid the foundations of a Palestinian national identity and strengthened their forces for the battles that lay ahead. Like Kanafani, you've argued that the vacillations of the traditional Palestinian leadership played a key role in the defeat, kowtowing as they did—at the St. James Conference, for example—to the collaborationist Arab kings, who had been put on their thrones by the British.

RK: Then as now, the Palestinian leadership was divided. They were stymied by their own inability to agree on an appropriate strategy—to mobilize the population and create a representative national forum, a popular assembly where these matters could be discussed. The British, unlike in India, Iraq, and parts of Africa, denied Palestinians any political access to the colonial state. So the argument for a people's assembly to break decisively with the structures of colonial control was very important.

TA: The other background condition for the Arab Revolt was the rise of fascism in Europe.

RK: From the moment the Nazis came to power, the whole situation changed for Jews in their relationship to the world and to Zionism. That's entirely understandable. It produced changes in Palestine too: Between 1932 and 1939, the Jewish proportion of the population rose from 16 or 17 percent to 31 percent. The Zionists suddenly had a viable demographic base for taking over Palestine, which they didn't have in 1932.

TA: The Palestinians became indirect victims of the European Judeocide.

RK: Absolutely. Palestinians are paying for the entire history of European Jew-hatred, going back to medieval times. Edward I expelling the Jews from England in 1290, the French expulsions in the following century, the Spanish and Portuguese edicts in the 1490s, the Russian pogroms from the 1880s, and finally the Nazi genocide. Historically, it has been a quintessentially European Christian phenomenon.

TA: What if there had been no Judeocide in Europe and the German fascists had been ordinary fascists without the obsession to wipe out the Jews?

RK: What a might-have-been. But look at the situation in 1939. There was already a Zionist project, with strong British imperial support, for reasons that had nothing to do with Jews or Zionism. It had to do with strategic interests. The Balfour Declaration was made by the man responsible for shepherding through the most antisemitic bill in British parliamentary history, the Aliens Act of 1905. The British ruling class didn't care for the Jews per se. They may have cared for their reading of the Bible, but what they cared about most was the strategic importance of Palestine and the Middle East as a gateway to India, long before 1917. That was what concerned them, from the beginning to the end. When they were forced to leave in 1948, they could do so because they'd already quit India in 1947 and didn't need Palestine in the same way. Had Hitler been assassinated, there would still have been a Zionist project, with British imperial backing. Zionism would still have tried to take over the entirety of the country, which was always its objective, and would still have tried to create a Jewish majority through ethnic cleansing and immigration. I couldn't speculate beyond that.

TA: But weren't there also anti-Zionist currents within the Jewish communities?

RK: Certainly, there were Jewish communists, Jewish assimilationists. The vast majority of the persecuted Jewish population of Eastern Europe who chose emigration went to the white-settler colonies: South Africa, Australia, Canada, New Zealand, and, above all, the United States; some also went to Argentina and other Latin American countries. These were the majority and that's where the bulk of the Jewish population of the world went, besides those who stayed in Europe.

Anti-Zionism was a Jewish project, up until Hitler. Before then, Zionists were a minority and their program was deeply contested in Jewish communities. But the Holocaust produced a kind of understandable uniformity in support of Zionism.

TA: Defeats usually have the effect of stopping everything for a time; then the resistance rises again, in different forms. But in the case of 1936–39, the defeat was immediately followed by the eruption of the Second World War—which started in China, though many call it a European war. What was the attitude of the Palestinian leadership in that period? In Indonesia, Malaysia, India, and parts of the Middle East, some sections of the nationalist movements said: "The enemy of our enemy is our friend, if only temporarily. Since our enemy is the British Empire, that means the Germans or the Japanese." In his book on Egypt, Anouar Abdel-Malek recounts how, when it appeared that Rommel might take Egypt, huge crowds gathered in Alexandria chanting, "Forward, Rommel, forward!" They wanted anyone but Britain. What was the attitude in Palestine?

RK: The attitude in Palestine was deeply divided. A minority faction of the leadership aligned themselves with the Germans, following the Grand Mufti. He had an extraordinary wartime career: The French kicked him out of Beirut, the British chased him out of Iraq when they reoccupied it in 1941, then they chased him out of Iran. He tried to go to Turkey, but the Turks wouldn't let him stay, so he ended up in Rome, and then Berlin. But most Palestinians did not adopt that line. Many joined the British Army and fought with the Allied forces. Of course, many leaders had been killed by the British, either on the battlefield or executed. Others were exiled. The British loved to exile their nationalist opponents to island possessions: Malta, the Seychelles, Sri Lanka, the Andamans. My uncle was sent to the Seychelles for a couple of years, together with other Palestinian leaders, then exiled to Beirut for several more years. And so the leadership for the most part understood that Britain could never be their friend. You can read my uncle's memoirs—he became virulently, venomously anti-British. He was always a nationalist and anti-British, but the degree to which the Revolt changed Palestinian views is remarkable. Previously, the leadership had always tried to conciliate the British, along the lines of many co-opted colonial elites. This changed with the crushing of the Revolt.

Ultimately, the defeat of the Revolt and then the Second World War left the Palestinians ill-prepared for what came after, when the two new superpowers—the US and the Soviet Union—supported Zionism, while on the ground the British collaborated with the Zionists and Jordanians to prevent the establishment of a Palestinian state. The Palestinians were not sufficiently organized to face the assault of the Zionist military, which began in November 1947, months before the mandate ended on May 15, 1948, when the UN partition was supposed to go into effect and the Arab armies joined the fray. By then, Zionist forces had taken Jaffa, Haifa, Tiberias, Safad, and dozens of villages, expelling around 350,000 Palestinians, and had already overrun much of what was to have been the Arab state under the UN Partition Plan. So the Palestinians were already defeated before the State of Israel was proclaimed and the so-called Arab–Israeli War began.

TA: We'll come to the role of the United States in all this. But how do you explain the Soviet Union's support for the Zionists, supplying them with Czech weapons in order to carry on fighting?

RK: Stalin turned on a dime, as you know. From being a staunch antinationalist and anti-Zionist power, the Soviet Union suddenly became an advocate of a Jewish state. This came as a huge shock to the Communist parties of the Arab world. There were several motivations, I think. It was certainly an effort to outbid the United States, and there was a sense that this might be a socialist country that would align with the Soviet Union. Stalin also wanted to undermine the British in the Middle East. Remember, he had spent his youth fighting in the south of what became the Soviet Union during the Russian Civil War, when the British were the primary supporters of the Whites—funding, arming, and training them. The British supported them with troops and fleets from the Baltic to the Caspian to the Black Sea. Early on, Stalin developed a great animosity toward Britain, and an obsession about the threat posed by British power to the southern regions of the USSR. And he now saw this as a moment in which the Soviet Union could undermine Britain's Arab puppet regimes in the region.

TA: It was a disastrous political intervention. But it didn't last too long.

RK: A couple of years. But yes, absolutely. If you look at the vote in the UN General Assembly, without the Soviet Union and their Belarusian and Ukrainian attachments, as well as the countries they influenced, the Americans would have had difficulty pushing through the partition resolution. They might have done it, but it could have led to a different outcome. And the Czech arms deal was crucial to Israel's victories against the Arab armies on the battlefield.

TA: That brings us to the Arab elites—the monarchies and sheikhdoms installed by Britain after the collapse of the Ottomans—their collaboration with the British, and their failure to help defeat this entity that the British Empire had created.

RK. The Egyptian, Jordanian, and Iraqi monarchies played the most important role here. They were subject to competing pressures, from above and below. On the one hand, the British had absolutely no desire to see a Palestinian state. They still had enormous hostility to the Palestinians, even as they had also become hostile to the Zionists because of the bloody campaign waged against them by the Irgun, the Stern Gang, and the Haganah at the end of the Second World War. Britain abstained on the UN partition resolution. A Jewish state would be established—there was nothing that could prevent that. But they hoped through their client regimes to balance its power and to maintain influence in a part of Palestine, thanks to Emir Abdullah of Transjordan, whose army was commanded by British officers.

On the other hand, there was the pressure of public opinion. The Arab world had long been concerned about Zionism. When I was researching this, I found hundreds of early newspaper articles about Palestine before World War I from Istanbul, Damascus, Cairo, and Beirut. There were volunteers from Syria and Egypt fighting in Palestine during the Arab Revolt. So these neighboring regimes came under popular pressure to do something about the catastrophe that was unfolding in Palestine in 1947–48, as the Zionists rapidly gained the upper hand and destitute refugees began arriving in Arab capitals. The British wanted the Jordanians to go in, of course—to annex the West Bank and East Jerusalem for themselves. Egypt and the other Arab countries were forced to intervene by their populations. But they did so in a half-hearted way, and only once the British had withdrawn.

This had a hugely radicalizing effect on the Arab junior officers involved, including Abdel Nasser. He wrote in his memoirs: We were not given the means to fight, and as we were fighting the Israelis, we were thinking of the corrupt British-controlled monarchy at home. Along with two close colleagues in the nationalist Free Officers group, Abdel Hakim Amer and Zakaria Mohyedin, Nasser was posted to Gaza and Rafah, and observed firsthand the anger of the rank-and-file soldiers against the high command in Cairo. He quotes a soldier who kept repeating with each new pointless order: "Shame, shame on us," in the drawn-out sarcastic intonation of the Egyptian countryside.[3] The war boosted the popularity of the Free Officers and ultimately led to the toppling of the monarchy in 1952. This was true with the Iraqis and the Syrians, too. Almost as soon as the war ended there was a series of coups in Syria, followed by the 1952 revolution in Egypt, and then Iraq in 1958. The military officers involved had all fought in Palestine.

TA: So Palestine was partitioned, but not according to the plan agreed by the United Nations.

RK: Ben-Gurion and the Zionist leadership wanted to take it all, they just didn't have the means at the time. So they settled for 78 percent.

TA: And there has been semi-continuous war since then. The first wave of refugees arrived in Gaza after the Nakba in 1948, including many of our friends. They had never lived in Gaza before.

RK: Eighty percent of the population of what is now the Gaza Strip are descended from refugees, most of whom arrived in 1948. There are populations from the Negev and other areas who were expelled even later. But 80 percent of Gaza's population originally came from elsewhere.

TA: Like much of my generation, I first learned of the scale of the Palestinian Nakba—the catastrophe—in 1967, after the Six-Day War. I was sent to visit the refugees by the Bertrand Russell Peace Foundation, which wanted us to produce an investigative report—as we had done in Vietnam for the International War Crimes Tribunal that Russell and Sartre had convoked. On that trip I met your cousin Walid Khalidi in his house in Beirut, which I will never forget. He sat me down and said: "Do you know what happened?" He told me about the massacre of Deir Yassin in April 1948. My eyes were coming out of my head. I couldn't believe that I hadn't known.

RK: Do you recall when this was?

TA: I think it must have been in July, a month after the 1967 Six-Day War. We met refugees in camps in Jordan, outside Damascus, and in Egypt, as well as politicians and intellectuals. Ironically, our translator was a Muslim Englishman, Faris Glubb, whose father, General Sir John Glubb, had been commander-in-chief of the Transjordanian Army. Faris was a rock-solid supporter of the Palestinian cause. Walid was very tickled by this fact. He was the one who first gave me a real tutorial on Palestinian history.

RK: He's very good at that. He's about to reach his ninety-ninth birthday, *inshallah*, in July.[4]

TA: I will never forget that afternoon in Beirut. And if people like me, growing up in a left-wing, pro-Arab, pro-Nasser family, didn't know about the Nakba at that time, then large numbers of people couldn't have had any idea.

RK: Absolutely. I am constantly struck by how poor a job the Palestinians did in publicizing their cause, starting in 1917 and going well beyond 1967. It's only really with the current generation that there has been any kind of a breakthrough. And this has not come from the political leadership, but from civil society—organizations like PACBI, the group calling for Boycott, Divestment, Sanctions, or the Institute for Palestine Studies that Walid founded, which has been working for decades. Finally, we're beginning to see the results. But this is in spite of the absence of any competent official effort. The PLO made a start on informational and diplomatic work in the 1970s and early 1980s, though it was still insufficient. Aside from that, the record has been dismal.

TA: How do you explain the persistent weakness of the modern Palestinian leadership? I know that the best people were killed.

RK: That's the first important point. Assassinating Palestinian leaders became an Israeli specialty. An Israeli author, Ronen Bergman, has a chilling book about this, *Rise and Kill First*. The title says it all. They have been very careful in picking out the ones they want to eliminate. Together with a few Arab regimes, it must be said: The Israelis have been helped in their efforts by the assassins of Libya, Iraq, and Syria. And the Israelis knew their targets. When they went to assassinate Abu Jihad in Tunis, they went straight past the home of Mahmoud Abbas. They didn't consider him a danger—on the contrary—so they kept him alive and have been using him ever since. This was also a British specialty.

But the problems of the Palestinian leadership go deeper. In the 1930s, it was in part a product of the Palestinian class structure—an out-of-touch landed elite with blinkered or naïve views on how to deal with the British. Since the 1960s, the lack of a global outlook on the part of successive generations of Palestinian leaders has been a major problem. If you look at other anticolonial movements—the Irish, the Algerians, the Vietnamese, or the Indians—they were led by people with a sophisticated understanding of the global balance of power, of the way imperial powers operate, and how to reach public opinion in the metropole. Nehru, Michael Collins, de Valera understood this. The Algerian leadership understood France. What they called the seventh *wilaya* or province of the FLN was in France. The Irish won in 1921 not only because they fought the British to a standstill, but also because they understood British and American politics and had extensive political and intelligence operations there. The Palestinian leadership has never had the same knowledge or skills. I hate to say this, it sounds self-denigrating, but it's true.

TA: How would you characterize the Palestinian elite in that early period? In *The Hundred Years' War on Palestine*, you give a wonderful sense of these Palestinian clans, the Khalidis and the Husseinis. Yours was more intellectual, more scholarly; the Husseinis tended to occupy practical leadership roles. Was this kind of class structure particular to Palestine, or did it exist in some form in other parts of the Arab world?

RK: The term used by my teacher, Albert Hourani, was "notables"—the politics of the notables.[5] He talked about families, rather than clans; these were not tribal populations. The same social structure prevailed throughout the Arab provinces of the Ottoman Empire; they were urban elites, involved in religion, law, and government; also, in many cases, they were landlords and involved in trade. This stratum was quite divorced from the popular classes, disdaining manual labor and, in many cases, commerce itself. It was imbricated in Ottoman politics for centuries, and before that, in the Mamluk Empire. Members of my family were involved in the Mamluk judiciary in the fourteenth and fifteenth centuries. This elite was well suited to the kind of administration you had under the Moguls, the Safavids, and the Ottomans. Some adapted to the modern era. Instead of religious training, they went to Malta or Istanbul, or to American missionary institutions. They acquired a modern education; instead of wearing a turban or a fez, they sported a top hat. But they were exquisitely ill suited to dealing with the British.

This social structure was completely destroyed in 1948. The material base of the class that had dominated Palestinian society for centuries disappeared. Landlords lost their lands, merchants lost their businesses, and so on. And with the odd exception, none of these elites re-emerged after 1948. Palestinian society was essentially revolutionized, in the way that many other Arab societies were by social revolution—in Iraq, Syria, Egypt, where the age-old elites and the landlord class were overthrown in the 1950s. Dynasties like the Azms in Damascus disappeared from politics. The same thing happened in Palestine because of the Nakba. In a sense, it opened the door to those from the educated middle class. The leadership of the PLO was not made up of people from old notable families. The only exception I can think of was Faisal Husseini: He was the only prominent Palestinian leader after 1948 who came from the old elite class, and he was the son of an outstanding military leader who was killed in battle in 1948.

TA: What happened to your own family at that point?

RK: The family was scattered. Some were traumatized by the experience and others were galvanized. My grandparents lost the family home at Tal al-Rish, near Jaffa, and became refugees. My uncles and aunts and cousins ended up between Jerusalem, Nablus, Beirut, Amman, Damascus, and Alexandria. As a result, I have cousins all over the Arab world and others in Europe and the US. Nevertheless, members of my family were among the lucky and privileged ones, as they had good educations thanks to my grandfather, and some of them had careers as professors, like my cousins Walid, Usama, and Tarif, or as writers and translators, like my aunt Anbara or my cousin Randa. My parents, who had been planning to return to Palestine after my father finished his PhD at Columbia, ended up having to stay in the US, which is why I was born here in New York, in 1948. My father then worked for the United Nations.

TA: Where did you go to school?

RK: I went to the UN International School in New York, and I also went to school in Korea. I studied history at Yale and did my DPhil at Oxford, with Hourani. So I was educated in three different places.

TA: And Palestine was absent in all these places.

RK: Yes. I've only lived in Palestine for short periods, a couple of years total. I lived in Libya for a few years when I was very young, and I lived in Lebanon for over fifteen years, in the 1970s and 1980s, teaching at the American University of Beirut. I've lived in other places, but most of my youth and more than half my life has been spent in the United States.

TA: To go back to the radical upheavals of the 1940s: As you were saying, the class structure changed all over the Arab world.

RK: With one categorical exception: the remaining monarchies. The old social order in Morocco has not changed, nor in Jordan or Saudi Arabia. At least, it didn't change in the same way.

TA: The British kept the monarchies on wherever they could. Churchill in particular loved them and even discussed the possibility of creating one for the Indian province of the Punjab.

RK: British colonialists loved to replicate their own aristocracy and their own system. They would find a landed gentry in places that had never known such a thing. The French preferred colonial republics.

TA: The other consequence of these radicalized middle-class upheavals was that the urban petit bourgeoisie gained access to the army, especially in Egypt, Syria, and Iraq. This was the basis of the revolutionary nationalist movements—in India, the native officer corps was limited to the second sons of the landed gentry. How did these transformations play out among the Palestinian communities, in the diaspora and in Palestine? Nasser was a great hero for the post-Nakba generation. And he did try, to be fair—it's not that he didn't try. I remember saying this to a Palestinian in Egypt, who replied with a joke: "Yes, Tariq, he tried, but, you know, he's like a bad clock. A clock says 'tick-tock' and moves forward. Nasser says 'tac-tic' and moves backward." In my view, the new generation of Palestinian leaders really came into its own after the Six-Day War, when they recognized that no Arab state was going to defend them and they had to fight for themselves. What would you say to that?

RK: My view of Abdel Nasser would be somewhat similar; one of my former students berated me the other day for criticizing him. But the point to stress is that I don't think Palestine was ever Nasser's priority, even in 1948. If you read his memoir, which was ghostwritten of course, it's clear that his obsession was Egypt. He was an Egyptian nationalist, understandably. Palestine was important, but it was never the priority. But to address the other question you ask: How did this new generation of Palestinian resistance leaders arise? It had started to coalesce before 1967, but the trauma of the Six-Day War had an enormous impact. As you say, it cemented the understanding that the Arab states weren't going to help. I think many believed that Nasser would—and this was the last straw. The successive defeats of 1948, 1956, and 1967 showed that the Arab states didn't have the means to defeat Israel, irrespective of whether they had the will to do so. Initiatives that had been brewing in Palestinian society led to the takeover of the

Palestinian Liberation Organization, which Nasser had established in 1964 in order to co-opt and control the rising tide of national fervor. In 1968 the PLO was taken over by independent Palestinian groups who were dissatisfied with Egyptian control. Fatah was the largest of these, and Arafat soon became PLO chairman. Once again, this was a movement from below against the co-opted elites, Ahmad Shukeiri and others, who originally ran the PLO. Shukeiri, by the way, was another member of the old upper class. But from this point on, there was a new generation of Palestinian leaders—Arafat, Hawatmeh, Habash, Abu Jihad, and others—who represent a different class, a different set of identities, to everything that went before.

One of Arafat's most important slogans was *al-qarar al-Filistini al-mustaqil*—independent Palestinian decision-making power. His insistence on Palestinian autonomy and self-determination was key to his popularity in this early period: "The Arab regimes don't control us." This was one of his relatively few successes, but a major one: keeping the PLO largely independent from the Arab powers who wanted to control the Palestinian movement, just as they have tried to do since the 1930s. During the Great Revolt, at the 1939 St. James Conference, in the debate over the UN partition resolution or the establishment of the PLO, the Arab regimes consistently tried to dominate the Palestine question, for their own benefit—in rivalry with one another, of course. They are still trying to do so, even as they look on impassively and do absolutely nothing as Gaza is martyred.

TA: You've already touched on another leading figure from this generation, Ghassan Kanafani. You write very movingly of him in *The Hundred Years' War on Palestine*. I met him once at a conference in Kuwait in 1966 and was bowled over.

RK: He was enormously charismatic. You read him now, and the charisma almost comes off the page. But if you met him . . . I only met him a couple of times. The man was extraordinary.

TA: I can't remember his exact words, which have since become famous, but I asked, "Is there any possibility of a negotiated settlement with these bastards?" And he said—I'll never forget his voice or his smile—"Tariq, explain to me how the neck negotiates with the sword." I laughed a lot. I said, that's a very brilliant analogy. He was a great intellectual, a writer as well as a political leader. He seemed to represent a whole culture. And so they killed him. Mossad blew him up, while he was traveling with his niece.

RK: Exactly. His literary works resonate to this day. My son Ismail adapted his novella *Returning to Haifa* for the stage, with Naomi Wallace. It's impossible to get a major theater in the US to show it, though it premiered in London at the Finborough Theatre. The adaptation was commissioned by the Public Theater in New York, but the board refused to allow it to be produced: They said Kanafani was a "terrorist." Yet in spite of the establishment censorship, his work is everywhere. To this day, the novellas are in print, as well as his plays, his poetry, his other writings, both in Arabic and in translation. Along with Mahmoud Darwish and Edward Said, I think he's the most important Palestinian intellectual of the twentieth century.

TA: This is what we were saying earlier: They know whom to kill.

RK: And whom not to kill.

TA: What led to Arafat and the team around him finally deciding to sell out at Oslo in 1993? Our friend Edward Said called it a "Palestinian Versailles"—a punitive peace.

RK: Edward was right, but he didn't know how right. In fact, it was far worse than Versailles. The turning point was 1988, when Arafat's team on the Palestinian National Council essentially capitulated to the Americans' conditions for entering bilateral dialogue—the Palestinians must renounce violence, something the Israelis were never asked to do, and accept partition, signing on to UN Resolution 242, which confined the issues to the outcome of the 1967 War. That UN resolution was drafted by Arthur Goldberg, Abba Eban, and Lord Caradon: Its authors were the great imperial powers and their Israeli client, though endorsed in the UN Security Council by the USSR. In fact, the Israelis didn't want the PLO to capitulate at that point. They were not interested in talking, no matter what the PLO accepted. They could agree to UNSC 242, accept the "two-state solution," renounce violence—and the Israelis still wouldn't talk to them, until Rabin finally broke the taboo in 1992.

Behind the PLO turn lay the outcome of the 1973 October War, when the Egyptian and Syrian regimes made clear that their interests were limited to their own territories occupied in 1967, Sinai and the Golan Heights. Beyond that, they didn't care. And this was made clear to the Palestinian leadership. I saw some of them coming back from Cairo. I was living in Beirut at the time and I was interpreting for a Palestinian-American delegation. They talked about their experience in Cairo with Sadat and how he made it clear that, this is it. This is what we're in for, and this is all we're in for. You guys take care of yourselves. He didn't say that in so many words . . .

TA: But that's what he meant and that's what they did.

RK: That's what the PLO leadership understood. And from that point on, they began to shift away from armed struggle and the liberation of Palestine toward negotiations for a so-called two-state solution. In 1974, at the Palestine National Council, they pushed through the first change to the wording. The PFLP and the bulk of the Fatah membership understood perfectly well what they were trying to do and opposed it.[6] It took the leadership years to get to the point where they were able to win the PNC's explicit approval for this program—to move the PLO from a position of liberation of all of Palestine, with a secular-democratic state for Muslims, Christians, and Jews in which everybody is equal, to a one-state-plus-multiple-Bantustans solution, which is what the US-brokered two-state solution has always meant in practice. That's what the Israelis have given us, little bits and pieces separated by huge swathes of illegal Israeli settlements. The Arafat leadership arguably accepted this in principle in 1974 and then moved, slowly but surely, toward winning over Palestinian public opinion and the movement.

TA: The other day Hillary Clinton entered the fray, adding her pebble to the mountain of lies that has been built around the "peace process." She basically said, "We offered the Palestinians everything at the Camp David Accords in 1978, but they turned us down. They could have had their own state by now." You know that phase intimately.

RK: One of my students, a scholar called Seth Anziska, wrote the best book on the long-term impact of Camp David.[7] I focused on the Madrid and Washington negotiations in *Brokers of Deceit*. The basic point is that Palestinian statehood and sovereignty, and an end to occupation and settlement, have never been on the table, ever, anywhere, at any stage, from any party, the United States or Israel or anybody else. At Camp David in 1979, "autonomy" was offered. At Madrid and

Washington, in 1991, we were only allowed to negotiate for "autonomy," or self-government under Israeli sovereignty; all we were told was that "final-status issues" would include discussion of these other things. But we know what the bottom line was. Rabin told us. In his last speech in 1995, just before he was assassinated for going too far, he explained how far he would actually go. He said: What we are offering the Palestinians is less than a state and we would maintain security control over the Jordan Valley. In other words, no self-determination, no sovereignty, no statehood. A one-state-multiple-Bantustans solution.

That was Israel's offer. And it never changed. Rabin was assassinated—he might have changed, you can speculate on that, if he had not been killed. But this is what he said in his last speech to the Knesset. And that was the bottom line for Ehud Barak in 2000, who negotiated with the PLO, unlike most other Israeli leaders. Rabin, Barak, and later Olmert were actually willing to negotiate—they were willing to put the sword to the neck, in Kanafani's inimitable expression. But what were they offering? Not statehood, not sovereignty, not self-determination, not an end to occupation, and not a removal of settlements. As for Clinton: one of the greatest liars in American politics and involved in multiple war crimes. She said that the students don't understand history. Well, what she's propagating is certainly not history. It's a completely distorted narrative which is false in almost every respect.

TA: Let's turn to Hamas. Is it accurate to say, as many of its opponents in the PLO insist, that it was created by Israel?

RK: No. Let me be very clear. Hamas emerged in 1987–88, in the situation we've just talked about. It grew out of the Islamist movement in Gaza, as a separate Palestinian extension of the Muslim Brotherhood in Egypt. This occurred just at the moment when Fatah and the PLO moved away from the goal of liberating the entirety of Palestine, as a secular-democratic state, to accepting the American–Israeli conditions laid out in UNSC 242, laying down arms, agreeing to a divided Palestinian statelet side-by-side with Israel. The PLO formally accepted this in 1987–88, which is precisely when Hamas emerged as a breakaway from the Islamist movement.

Now, were they encouraged by the Israelis? Yes, of course they were. Israel saw the PLO as its chief nationalist opponent, the primary danger. Any dissident movement which undermined the wall-to-wall support of the Palestinians for the PLO was welcome to Israeli intelligence. Of course it was. Two Israeli specialists, Shaul Mishal and Avraham Sela, wrote a good book on Hamas which talks about this.[8] There was also an excellent Reuters article, which went into detail about how the Israeli intelligence services manipulated and supported the Islamist movement in Gaza. Everything else was shut down—every expression of Palestinian identity, even the Palestine Red Crescent—but not the Islamists. They operated freely. When the

Israelis needed somebody to beat up PLO demonstrators on the Birzeit campus, in the West Bank, they would bus Islamists from Gaza across Israel, equipped with tire irons and batons, to beat the living daylights out of pro-PLO demonstrators. Friends told me about kids having their arms broken by these guys. The Islamists were allowed to operate without being arrested, without being interfered with, as no other Palestinian civil society organizations were.

When Hamas emerged, the Israeli occupation authorities were divided at first, because Hamas produced its notorious antisemitic charter and launched operations against Israeli soldiers and settlers in Gaza, after the start of the Intifada in December 1987. There was a debate within Israeli intelligence and the military: Do we really want to continue supporting these people or not? But at different times, they were, if not supported, at least allowed to operate, for divide-and-rule reasons, by the Israeli intelligence services that controlled the Gaza Strip. I just saw a wonderful film called *Gaza Ghetto* made by Joan Mandell [with Pierre Björklund and Per-Åke Holmquist] in 1984, which talks about what the Gaza Strip was like under Israeli occupation up to that point. She lived in Palestine at the time. The Israeli occupation controlled everything, as it controls everything in the West Bank today. There were attempts at resistance, obviously, some of which were successful, others not. But over time, Hamas turned into a resistance movement, and then the Israelis were not so happy with it. But they went back to supporting it in the last few years, under Netanyahu, because they thought they could use Hamas to pacify the Gaza Strip, with cash coming from the Gulf countries, Qatar in particular.

TA: But that turned out not to be the case.

RK: It didn't work out so well for them.

TA: We now have the irony that the so-called secular-democratic PLO is 100 percent or 99.9 percent collaborationist with the Israelis, that there is no Palestinian "Authority," that effectively, the IDF issues the orders and the Fatah-run PA carries them out. While the Muslim Brotherhood–style Islamist organization, Hamas, has become the leadership of what we have to call, and what is in fact, today's Palestinian resistance.

RK: The terrible irony is that what Arafat and his colleagues did in accepting the Oslo Accords, and in moving almost the entire national movement into an Israeli-controlled prison in the occupied territories, first of all, hollowed out the PLO itself. Today the PLO doesn't really exist, except as a shell. That leadership now operates through this puppet quisling Palestinian Authority, which is a subcontractor for the occupation. It doesn't have an independent existence. It has no authority, no jurisdiction, and no sovereignty. It's simply an arm of occupation, one of several. The Arafat–Abbas leadership thereby hollowed out what used to be the core of the national movement, which was the PLO. There is no PLO to speak of now. There is a Palestinian Authority, a bureaucracy which has governing power over the civil lives of Palestinians in part of the West Bank, though only a small part. The majority of the West Bank, so-called Area C, is controlled directly by the Israeli military. At most, the Palestinian Authority has a presence in 20 to 30 percent of the West Bank, in terms of responsibility for public education, health, and so on. But Israel is the sovereign power over the entirety of the occupied West Bank and occupied Arab East Jerusalem. It is the occupying power. It is the security power. It controls the population registry, entry and exit, everything to do with funding. It controls the PA security services. They do what the Israelis want. The Palestinian people want to be protected from the occupation and settlers, but the PA's people serve as agents of the occupation. They serve the enemy. So, yes: This is a tragedy for the secular-democratic, non–Muslim Brotherhood elements of the Palestinian national movement.

TA: After Oslo, *New Left Review* described Fatah's trajectory as a lurch from fantasy maximalism to ignominious minimalism, with no attempt to define and fight for an equitable solution in between.[9] There are still some in the PLO who are resisting. Hanan Ashrawi has been stronger than the others, and I'm sure there must be others waiting for some alternative.

RK: There are many people, including people involved in the PLO/Fatah, and even some involved with the

Palestinian Authority, though not many, who still have an independent position and who oppose the PA's collaborationist nature. You can see very clearly from a series of public opinion polls how broadly despised Abu Mazen (Mahmoud Abbas) is, how hated the PA is. This in spite of the fact that it provides the salaries for a huge proportion of the population of the occupied territories. There are tens of thousands of security personnel, tens of thousands of government employees, teachers, people in the healthcare sector, who are on the Palestinian Authority payroll and are entirely dependent on it for their livelihoods. In spite of that, the PA is loathed by overwhelming majorities of the population. That's perfectly clear.

The interesting thing is that Hamas's popularity has not always been as great as some people think, whether in Gaza, where they were growing increasingly unpopular before October 7, or even in the West Bank, where they are more popular than in Gaza simply because people have not been governed by them. But many of those under their rule in the Gaza Strip took a dim view of Hamas. It depends on the poll, who's asking and whom they ask. Public sentiment is not static; it goes up and down over time. But the question of the degree of Hamas's popular support really should be asked much more carefully than it is. People assume, because a lot of young people were swept away by enthusiasm after October 7, that it is still the view of most people today, eight months later. I don't think that's necessarily the case. Hamas is seen as deserving credit for inflicting a military defeat on Israel, the likes of which it has never suffered. Israel took a beating on some battlefields in 1948 and it suffered a severe military setback at the beginning of the 1973 war, before the Americans came to its rescue. But since 1948, Israel has never had to fight for days on its own territory. It took them four days to retake the military bases and the numerous communities that were overrun by Hamas and its allies on October 7. That had not happened before. The highest Israeli civilian death toll since 1948 was inflicted by the attack of October 7. (Israeli propaganda claims "the highest since the Holocaust," but that's not true: 2,000 Israeli civilians and 4,000 troops died in 1948.) But Israel has never suffered an intelligence failure or a military defeat of this magnitude, even in 1973. So many people give Hamas credit for this, even though they may have reservations about them on other counts.

TA: The Israelis knew what was going on in 1973. The Americans were telling them.

RK: They knew, or they found out somewhat belatedly, but they didn't react fast enough, out of arrogance or hubris. They had spies in Egypt. They had spies everywhere. They had people telling them, "Wait, wait, they're just doing exercises." Even if 1973 was as big a shock, with Syria taking the Golan Heights, there were few Israeli civilian casualties. This needs to be said again and again about October 7: In addition to the atrocities, which definitely took place, the highest civilian death toll that Israel has ever suffered since 1948 occurred on those four days at the beginning of this attack. This is something Palestinians have to take on board, if they want to understand why Israel is so savage in its collective punishment of Gaza. It's not just the military defeat and intelligence failure. It's not just about restoring the tarnished honor and shattered "deterrence" of the army. It's a visceral desire for revenge, retribution for the traumatic suffering of a large number of Israeli civilians. Not just those killed or captured: Entire communities were emptied and still haven't been repopulated, eight months later. This is fundamental if we want to understand what motivates the ferocity of Israeli behavior. There is an underlying logic to it that goes back to the launching of the Zionist project. Every settler-colonial project must behave ferociously, to establish itself at the expense of the indigenous population. But what we have witnessed for the past eight months is on a scale never seen before, even in 1948.

We are fully aware that since October 7, at least twenty-five times as many Palestinians have been killed as Israelis, with a huge proportion of them civilians, women, children, the elderly, medical and aid workers, journalists, academics. The world is now fully conscious of the trauma this is producing. But some have not yet fully integrated the degree to which Israeli society has been affected by the impact of those first four days that it took the Israeli military to relieve the besieged headquarters of the Gaza Division, to retake the Erez crossing point, the multiple military bases that had been captured and a dozen communities along the Gaza frontier. It took them until October 10. The shock to Israel is going to last for a very long time, just as the trauma of what is being done to Gaza now will affect Palestinians everywhere for many years to come. Not just Palestinians in Gaza, or people like me and my friends and students who have family in Gaza, or know people there. Every Palestinian is affected by this trauma, and many others besides.

TA: As we've discussed, none of the previous tragedies of Palestinian history had this impact on public opinion globally, certainly not in the United States. And yet, watching the encampments being set up on over a hundred American campuses is quite astonishing to me. I heard your fine speech to the protesting students at Columbia the other day. It's as if October 7 has brought about a generational shift, as far as Israel and Palestine are concerned. A significant layer of young people, including thousands of young Jews, like the ones who occupied Grand Central Station in New York, want nothing to do with this monster entity which kills at will. People see what Israel is doing, and they are saying that it's too much, it's unacceptable, it's genocide. And this is really rattling the mainstream media and the politicians. Do you think this will last? And, linked to that, how would you explain why Washington has become so utterly craven? In *Brokers of Deceit*, you provide a sober but very sharp analysis of the US role in the Middle East, particularly under Clinton and Obama, showing that while Washington claims to be an impartial mediator, seeking to advance an evenly balanced "peace process," in fact it is highly partial, acting as "Israel's lawyer" and its main backer. Nevertheless, when American interests were at stake, earlier administrations were prepared to crack the whip. Truman maintained an arms embargo against all belligerents in 1948; after Suez, Eisenhower told Ben-Gurion to get out of Gaza and the Sinai within two weeks or face sanctions; in August 1982, Reagan yelled at Begin to stop bombing Beirut; Bush Senior threatened to withhold $50 billion to get Israel to the negotiating table. The current layer, Democrats and Republicans alike, show absolutely no willingness to put on any pressure at all. Biden—"Genocide Joe" as the students have dubbed him—is the worst of the lot. Trump will be no better. Secretary of State Blinken dances like a tame monkey to all Netanyahu's tunes. Has the monkey become the organ-grinder? Why and how has it gone so far?

RK: It's actually a hard question to answer. We beat out our brains, trying to understand the degree to which they have become worse than complicit. They've become mouthpieces for every trashy piece of Zionist propaganda. The president and his appalling spokespeople, Admiral Kirby and the awful Matthew Miller, sound like Netanyahu's press attachés—like the worst Israeli propagandists, nakedly espousing an Israeli narrative on point after point. Today they admitted that the US is helping the Israelis try to hunt down and kill the Hamas leadership, that it provided intelligence for the hostage rescue that killed nearly 300 Palestinians. The RAF has flown almost daily surveillance missions over the Gaza Strip. America and Britain, its bloodshot adjutant, are participating directly in the slaughter, not just supplying weapons, money, and UN vetoes, but doing the intelligence and propaganda work for this genocide. You used the word "craven." This is worse than that. There are words in Arabic for it that I can't translate. The degree to which this administration has inhabited an Israeli perspective, from Biden through Blinken to Sullivan on down, marks it out.

It's true that in a couple of top leadership positions there are people who will not and do not repeat that rhetoric. The secretary of defense, Austin, and Burns, the head of the CIA, have not; nor have others, who know better. But they don't have any purchase within the administration on this question. I would guess that most career professionals who serve in the State Department, in the military, and in the so-called intelligence community—I love that term, intelligence "community"—know perfectly well that what Israel is doing is both futile and harmful to American interests; indeed, how harmful it is to any rational understanding of Israel's interests. But they have no voice in Biden's administration.

Part of this has to do with the generational divide that you mentioned. The US is ruled today by an aged clique, a gerontocracy, that was indoctrinated in the 1960s and 1970s with the myth of the connection between the Holocaust and the establishment of Israel.

Schumer, Pelosi, Biden, Trump: These are old people. Their consciousness was formed at the time of the 1967 War. And since then, they have never opened their minds, they have never had access to anything but a poisonous narrative that paints Israel in the most gleaming colors and the Palestinians in the darkest ones—the idea that Israel is always in existential danger, the Cossacks are always at the door; that the Holocaust could be repeated; that Israel represents a flower of Western civilization in a desert of Arab barbarism—a bunch of racist tropes that Israel, and the Zionist movement before it, successfully sowed throughout the West. Biden has not expressed the slightest sympathy for the 14,000 Palestinian children who have been killed by US bombs. He has no feeling of shame, no sense of the dimensions of the horrific genocide that he and his administration are helping to perpetrate. And the people around him mirror that, obviously. They're insulated.

How long can this continue? I don't know. I see no sign of it stopping. They have now dimly begun to deduce that Israel is harming its and their own interests, and they're trying to slow them down. But they have had no purchase with the Israelis so far. And if I were Netanyahu and my political survival depended on the continuation of the war, the Americans feebly bleating and threatening to delay an arms shipment or two would be no reason to stop it. He'll go on for as long as he wants, correctly assessing that the Americans are more bark than bite, and that any bite would be a toothless nip. If they were serious, the US could say, we'll stop all arms shipments, unless Israel accepts the ceasefire plan that the CIA chief, Burns, has drafted for them. It could sponsor a Security Council resolution demanding a ceasefire under specific provisions of the UN Charter, which would force Israel to stop tomorrow. They won't do that. To go back to what you said: This was something that Reagan himself was willing to do, in August 1982. The Israelis only stopped bombing Beirut because Reagan yelled at Begin, and half an hour later they called the bombing off. We were sitting there in Beirut, under Israeli bombardment, and suddenly it stopped, essentially because of a phone call from the US president to the Israeli prime minister. Biden hasn't done that.

TA: Mearsheimer and Walt were vilified for their book on the Israel lobby, called antisemites and so forth.[10] But the case they put for how American foreign policy is run on that level seems pretty strong today.

RK: The amusing thing is that, in spite of all the vilification and the slanders, *The Israel Lobby and US Foreign Policy* fast became a bestseller, and it is still selling very well. I know the authors, they're both friends of mine; I believe that with the latest war there has been a bump in sales, a decade and a half after it was published. I think it was a sound analysis. I don't think it was comprehensive enough because it only talked about the lobby groups on Capitol Hill, as well as the Christian Zionists and the neocons, and the lobby's vigilantes in the media and academia. However, there's a whole ecosystem that has extended to important elements of the American military, tech, and biomedical sectors, which are closely integrated with their Israeli equivalents. Enormously important parts of the US economy are linked to these sectors in Israel and these are powerful forces in American society. They own Congress, in the sense that their contributions keep elected politicians in office—Silicon Valley, biotech, finance, the military sector in particular. The imbrication of the US security-military-industrial complex with that of Israel is seamless, as is the imbrication of Israel's defense and intelligence networks with those in India, the Emirates, and a few other places. I don't think this is fully accounted for in *The Israel Lobby*, partly because some of this has emerged subsequent to publication of their book.

TA: Let's come to the subject of the present Arab elites, who are carrying on even more blatantly than they did after the Nakba. Prior to October 7, the Saudis were on the verge of recognizing Israel.

RK: They still are.

TA: They still are. And the Gulf States remain imperial petrol stations, with enormous amounts of money. Jordan has been a US–Israeli protectorate for a very long time. The Egyptian masses were brutally defeated by the army. I did think there might be more protests in the Arab world—and the only thing that could change the mood there would be mass uprisings. But apart from

Yemen, not too much. There have been pro-Gaza demonstrations, but so far not on the scale of the anger displayed in Britain and the US.

RK: I think there are at least two things to say here. The first thing is that there is, and has always been, a deep sympathy with Palestine among the Arab peoples, throughout the Arab world, from the Gulf to the Atlantic. This hasn't changed. It's gone up and down a little bit, but it hasn't gone away. But these people are facing other critical issues. If you live in a state that's been destroyed—like Libya, Syria, Iraq, Yemen, Sudan, Lebanon—by civil war or intervention by the imperial powers and their clients, you have other concerns. Iraq still doesn't have twenty-four-hour electricity, twenty-one years after the American occupation—and it's one of the greatest oil producers in the world. Palestine is important, but electricity and not being killed by the regime—or by this or that army faction—is also important. This is the situation in half a dozen Arab countries: different stages of civil war-cum-proxy war, with all the great powers involved.

The second thing is that, almost without exception, from the Gulf to the Atlantic, you don't have regimes that allow public opinion to express itself. There are jackboot dictatorships, "Le Pouvoir" in Algeria, the most absolutist monarchies since Louis XIV, which allow virtually no dissent beyond a tiny space, and if you go beyond it, you will be tasered and tortured, you will be arrested and your family will suffer. So, you're right, no protests in the Arab world have risen to the level of what we've seen in London and New York, or in some parts of the Global South, Indonesia and Pakistan. That's partly because the Arab masses have been cowed by the cattle prods and tortures inflicted on them since the so-called Arab Spring. They were brought back to order by America's clients, in particular the Saudis and the Emiratis, with vast infusions of cash and support for the most hardline security measures. One can't entirely blame the people for not being willing to raise their heads above a certain point over this issue.

In some places, however, the situation is critical—in Jordan, for example, and in a few other countries, under the surface. But I don't see this leading to the democratic transitions that would be necessary for these countries to play an active, positive role. Their rulers are more concerned about what Washington and Tel Aviv may say than about their own people. They don't represent their people's views in any shape or form. They're tied to Israel by so many visible and invisible ties. The antimissile defenses of the Emirates were provided by the Israeli subsidiary of Raytheon, which means that the first line of Israel's antimissile surveillance against Iran is in Jabal Ali, in Abu Dhabi, not Jabal al-Sheikh (Mount Hermon), in the occupied Golan Heights. The UAE depends entirely on Israel for its security against missile attack. There are variations of that arrangement in Jordan, Egypt, and other Arab countries. In Morocco, the royal bodyguards have been trained by Mossad for the past fifty or sixty years, since the time of King

Hassan II. The Israeli defense connection is generations-old in the case of Jordan, Morocco, and Egypt, and is well established in several of the Gulf countries, too.

TA: There was some hope expressed early on that Hezbollah, with the backing, quietly or publicly, of the Iranian regime, might open up a second front and relieve the pressure on Hamas. But that didn't happen.

RK: I think Hamas was wrong to expect it. They probably expected far more sustained responses from other Palestinians in the occupied territories and hoped that Hezbollah, as well as other Iran-allied militias and perhaps Iran itself, would be much more vigorous in reacting to Israel's counter-response to October 7. It's a perfect example of how little they understand of the world. For all their acumen in other respects, the leaders who organized this assault have what I would call tunnel vision. I think they believed that there would be an uprising throughout the Arab world. I don't have a lot of evidence for that assertion, but they were certainly disappointed by the reaction. And Hezbollah's response has been what I would call "performative." It's had a significant effect on Israel: In seven months it's killed at least fifteen Israeli soldiers and eleven Israeli civilians, according to Israeli sources, and it's led to the evacuation of the entire border region—tens of thousands have been forced to leave their homes.

But while it may still explode into a full-scale war, so far it's been tit for tat, very measured and controlled.

This is a function of what anybody with eyes to see could have told the boys in the tunnels, which is that Iran did not invest in building up Hezbollah's capabilities for the sake of Hamas. It did so in order to create a deterrent to protect Iran and Lebanon against Israel—that's the only reason. The idea that Hezbollah and the Iranians would shoot every arrow in their quivers to support Hamas, in a war Hamas started without warning its allies—it beggars belief that anybody could think that would be the case. Iran is a nation-state that has national interests, which are restricted to regime preservation, self-defense, and raison d'état. You can talk about Islam, ideology, and the "axis of resistance" until you're blue in the face. I will tell you: Raison d'état, regime protection—that's what they care about, and that's why they backed the buildup of Hezbollah's capacity. And they're not going to shoot that bolt. There was no possibility under any circumstances of their doing that to support Hamas. If, heaven forbid, a full-scale war erupts, it will be because of a miscalculation, or an accident, or an irrational move by Netanyahu, not a decision by Hezbollah.

Hezbollah is a Lebanese party. It has an Iranian patron, but it is acutely attuned to the fact that the Lebanese public will turn against it if its operations against Israel provoke a massive retaliation against Lebanon—which would not be directed against just Hezbollah but also, as in the 2006 war, against Lebanon's infrastructure. The Israelis have always punished the host country in order to force it to force the resistance to stop doing whatever it was doing. They bombed Jordan, they bombed Syria, in order to force those regimes to stop the Palestinians. They weren't just trying to stop the Palestinians themselves, but also to stop whichever Arab country it was from hosting and supporting the Palestinians. They would do that to Lebanon, to force it to stop Hezbollah. And Hezbollah knows that, and the Lebanese know it, too. I don't understand how the leaders of Hamas didn't understand that. It shows a detachment from reality and a flawed strategic sense which is really quite disturbing. Since October 7 they have dramatically upended the stagnant status quo in Palestine, and have shown themselves highly adept at waging guerrilla warfare—at an unspeakable price, let it be said. But ultimately, war is an extension of politics by other means, and they have not projected a clear, strategic, unified Palestinian political vision to the world. I don't think people are saying these kinds of things, hard as they are to say. But they should be. They should be.

TA: I agree with you entirely. Turning to the future, what is the Israeli plan for Gaza? Are they trying to create another Nakba: destroy the strip, sell it off to their own people, and turn more Palestinians into refugees? That is what seems to be the case. Or will someone intervene to stop this from happening? The Americans certainly won't—that's become very clear.

RK: Unlike at other critical moments in its history, Israel doesn't have a unified elite and there is no clear-cut position on these issues today. In 1948, Ben-Gurion dominated Israeli politics; even in 1956, he prevailed over Sharett and he did what he wanted in launching the Suez War. Episode by episode, whether they did well or did badly, they at least knew what they wanted to do. There was a cohesive, unified sense of Israel's interests, even after the 1967 War, when they couldn't quite decide—should we keep it all?—they had a cohesive leadership. The military and political leaderships operated in sync throughout most of Israel's history. That's not the case today. I don't think there is a clear Israeli vision of what to do. Netanyahu has very little idea of what he wants strategically. What he wants personally is a continuation of the war with no clear end strategy. That serves his narrow political interest: staying in power, not having an election, and not going on trial.

Other factions within his government have different views. The military and intelligence establishment is not cohesive. Just recently a former chief of staff came out and said the war has to end. You've never had former Israeli chiefs of staff saying this in wartime; Aviv Kohavi just said it.

Other former generals and intelligence chiefs have said similar things. The Israeli elite is divided, with good reason, over how to end the war, over what to do in Gaza on the day after, if it ever comes. At the beginning, it was clear that they hoped they could complete the Nakba and expel large numbers of people—into Egypt, and possibly also from the West Bank into

Jordan. And they sent their errand boy, Blinken, to do their dirty work for them—going to the Egyptians, to the Jordanians, and to the Saudis and begging them, please, could you allow this to happen? The participation of the American government in an Israeli plan to further ethnically cleanse Palestine is one of the most despicable episodes in American history. It will be a mark of shame on Blinken and Biden for the rest of time. In 1948, Washington didn't want ethnic cleansing, though Truman allowed it to happen and did nothing to uphold the UN partition resolution he had twisted so many arms to get. This is different and much worse. This is Washington actively supporting Israel in genocide and actively trying to broker its ethnic cleansing of a part of Palestine.

But if the Israeli leadership had a clear view of what they wanted at the beginning—devastate Gaza and complete the Nakba—I don't think they have a clear view now. What seems likely to ensue is some form of Israeli occupation, which is an outcome that nobody, including the Israelis themselves, should desire. I wouldn't want to occupy Gaza if I were them. Their last occupation, up to 2005, wasn't so successful. Think what they had to cope with then, from the Hamas of the early 2000s and other groups with capabilities a fraction of what they are today. I don't think there are any good options, frankly, from an Israeli perspective. I don't think there's been a clear leadership decision on this. That may be wrong, but that's my impression from the outside, reading the Israeli press. In spite of their overwhelming power, they have put themselves in a hopeless strategic situation.

TA: A terrible historical irony. After the Six-Day War in 1967, Isaac Deutscher gave an interview to *New Left Review*.[11] He had broken with Israel decisively and sent a message to Ben-Gurion, whom he knew, warning of disaster if the occupation was not ended. He described Israelis as the Prussians of the Middle East—a succession of victories breeding blind reliance on their own force of arms, chauvinistic arrogance, and contempt for other peoples—and recalled the lesson the Germans drew from their experience: "Man kann sich totseigen!" You can triumph yourself to death.

RK: Well, Ben-Gurion learned that. He was worried after the 1967 War that Israel would wallow in triumphalism and fail to take the opportunity the war offered to obtain a settlement favorable to Israel and Zionism. He was, of course, right. The sad thing about so many of these leaders is that they learn too late. So you have Ehud Olmert talking about things that he never talked about when he was prime minister, or Ben-Gurion saying things in his dotage that he never said before, or former Israeli generals or heads of Mossad and Shin Bet, full of wisdom after they've retired. I had a wonderful encounter with Yehoshafat Harkabi, chief of Israeli military intelligence in the 1950s, who wrote two seminal books that were blueprints for the demonization of the PLO. He served not just as chief of military intelligence, he was the lead propagandist in the West for a negative vision of the PLO. When I met him in his old age, the man had shifted completely and had written a series of books criticizing Israel. It often happens too late with these people. The same with Jimmy Carter. Why didn't you say this when you were president?

TA: Exactly.

RK: The best ex-president the United States ever had. But I'd like to finish answering your first question, asking what has changed and what has not. I grew up in a world, as I said, in which the Zionist narrative was the only game in town and was believed blindly by almost everybody. That's not the case today, as we've been discussing. There's a vigorous contestation of the Zionist narrative, within the Jewish community in particular, with an interesting generational divide. That's entirely new—and very important.

What has not changed, and what our grandchildren still have to contend with, is the unwavering support of the rulers of the imperial powers for the Zionist project. Especially the United States and Britain, from the First World War onward, and France and Germany after the Second World War. That is in many ways the biggest problem, to my way of thinking. If you accept the settler-colonial framework of analysis, then the metropole is as important as the settler colony. Israel is not a typical settler colony, by any means; it's also a national project, with a significant Biblical dimension, and a refuge from persecution. No other settler colony was a refuge from persecution to such a degree—the Puritans and other religious dissidents, like the Quakers, who came to North America, certainly experienced repression, but not on the same scale. Basically, this combination of characteristics is unique to the Israeli project. But the core of it, the settler-colonial core of it, relates to a metropole. And the elites in that metropole, unfortunately, have barely changed from the time when I was a child. The new generations are going to have to deal with this.

TA: A number of Israeli scholars and archaeologists, including Israel Finkelstein, have shown that the heroic stories of the Old Testament account—the Exodus, the royal lineage of the Book of Kings—were largely an "invented tradition," borrowings that were constructed as a court ideology in a later period. The Hebrew editions of Shlomo Sand's books, *The Invention of the Jewish People* and *The Invention of the Land of Israel*, have been bestsellers in Israel. But this has had negligible impact on the hold of the national ideology over the majority of the population.

RK: On nationalism, Gellner, Hobsbawm, and Benedict Anderson were right: It doesn't matter what the historical realities were, it's what people believe that counts. Finkelstein and other excellent Israeli archaeologists have blown to pieces much of the Biblical foundation of Zionism, to very little political effect. I think we have to look at the power of those Biblical myths, irrespective of their baselessness from a historical and archaeological perspective—their resonance over generations, over centuries, and not only among Jews. It's equally important that they have resonated among Christians. British Protestants are ultimately responsible for the Balfour Declaration, rooted in their belief in these same myths. Lord Shaftesbury was a Zionist in the 1830s, before the first Jewish Zionists, for religious reasons.

TA: But Israeli barbarism, as we're seeing it, is beginning to dent some of these myths, is it not?

RK: There may be a reckoning. Christian Zionism is primarily a Protestant phenomenon; it's much less prevalent among Catholic populations. That reading of the Bible—the "gathering of Israel" as a precursor to the Second Coming and the Last Judgment, the Revelation of Saint John the Divine—is essentially a Protestant reading. And in many of the more liberal Protestant denominations in the US, there is a growing understanding of the danger of that reading and how false it is in terms of Christian values. You see a parallel shift among Jews, who say that this has nothing to do with the Jewish tradition we want to uphold. We don't want to destroy people as the Israelites destroyed Amalek. We don't believe in the version of Judaism that animates many of the settlers and the right wing of the Israeli political spectrum—which stretches from the far right to the center left, by the way. They believe this stuff, about destroying the Amalekites as enemies of Israel. Netanyahu has cynically embraced that exterminationist logic, in a literalist reading of the Book of Saul: "Remember what Amalek has done to you." A majority of the Knesset, sixty-four members, are backing a government headed by a man who has said this again and again. Yet that's not what a large proportion of the Jewish community in the US believe.

TA: Now, lastly, to your own university, Columbia.

RK: It will cease to be my own university when I retire at the end of June.

TA: But you will still be associated in some way.

RK: I'll just be a former faculty member, teaching some courses as a nonmember of the faculty—or as "contingent" faculty, as we have come to call them.

TA: Might they do away with the "terrorist" name altogether, the Edward Said Professorship?

RK: I have no idea what will happen with that. There are donors and descendants of donors who will, I assume, insist that there continue to be a chair and that someone qualified should hold it. I have no idea. The campaign in the United States against Middle East Studies in general, and studies on Palestine in particular, is virulent and spans the political spectrum. And we now have the New

York City Police Department joining unprincipled politicians in the hue and cry, shamefully echoed by university administrators, about outside agitators and incitement by faculty members, including myself. So I don't know what will happen. When people ask me these kinds of questions, I say that the job description of a historian does not include predicting the future.

TA: You dedicated your last book to your grandchildren, which we oldies tend to do. [*Laughter*]

RK: Let the record show both of us laughing heartily.

TA: You expressed the hope that they would see a better world. What is the biggest difference between the world you grew up in and the world they're growing up in?

RK: I grew up in a world where there was no Palestinian voice—in the Arab world, in the public sphere in the West; none at all. It didn't exist. Palestinians didn't exist. My four grandchildren are growing up in a time when there are quite vigorous voices for Palestine, all over the world. So that's an element of change for the better. I grew up in a world in which the Zionist narrative was completely hegemonic and Israel was fulsomely described as "a light unto the nations." That is no longer the case. Today it is widely, and rightly, seen as a pariah state because of its own genocidal actions. These are among the few good things that have happened in these very bad times.

2.

January 9, 2026

Tariq Ali: Here we are again, Rashid, witnessing yet another ceasefire that never was a ceasefire and never was intended to be one as far as the Israelis and the Americans were concerned. My own feeling is that it was designed more as a fig leaf to cover the nakedness of the Arab states in the region: something to lure the resistance into disarming and to give the media something to cling to. But literally today the BBC has been forced to admit that the bombing of Gaza by Israel has never stopped since the ceasefire was announced. So even the mainstream media are now being forced to acknowledge the reality of the situation—even as grotesque celebrations take place in the Knesset between Trump and the Israelis, each congratulating the other on what they've achieved. There's something very weird about world politics at the moment, and what they're doing in Gaza is spreading all over the world, including in the US heartland, where IDF-trained ICE gangsters are now executing people in the streets. Why do you think Hamas agreed to this false ceasefire?

Rashid Khalidi: I think you put your finger on something when you said it was meant as a fig leaf for the Arab regimes. I think it was also meant as a sop to Western governments that are increasingly embarrassed in the face of public opinion, which has become overwhelmingly critical of Israel and much more sympathetic than ever before to the Palestinians. Despite this popular shift, these governments nevertheless remain unwilling to cut their ties with Israel. Sales of weapons to Israel from the UK, from Germany, from France, and obviously from the United States, are absolutely essential to this continued slaughter in Gaza, which, as you say, has been ongoing ever since the so-called ceasefire. They kill several people every day. They bomb every day. They shell every day. Their drones are in the air constantly attacking people. And of course it's not just Western governments. Arab states like Saudi Arabia, Egypt, and the UAE are totally complicit and actively facilitating the ongoing destruction of Gaza, despite their populations' overwhelming opposition. It's humiliating for them. This embarrassment of these Arab regimes was such that they were actually putting considerable pressure on the United States to do something. And so they did something. And that something that they did was to announce a fake ceasefire, as you put it.

But you put your finger on something else, as well, because what Israel has been doing in Gaza for more than two years now, with complete impunity, is a sort of a template for Trump's actions over the past year. He just said yesterday, I don't care about international law.

Well, neither do the Israelis. Discrimination, proportionality—the bases of international law where casualties among civilians are concerned—have been thrown out the window by the Israelis. And the United States is doing the same with international law generally. Its behavior in the world increasingly seems to be modeled on the kind of swaggering aggression that Israel is so proud of in its dealings with Syria, Lebanon, Palestine, Iran, and other countries. So I think these are peas in a pod, as it were, the United States and Israel. Rogue states operating outside any boundaries, even the boundaries of realism. We're not talking about the boundaries of international law anymore. We're talking about realism. We're talking about the limits that one would normally expect any state to pay attention to in terms of its own self-interest.

There are also parallels between the domestic and the international approaches of these two regimes, the Trump regime and the Netanyahu regime. The way they treat their domestic publics reflects their adventures abroad. You have Israeli police shooting people right and left, Jewish Israeli citizens and, of course, Palestinian citizens of the State of Israel. And just in the last two days in Minneapolis and Portland, ICE has shot three people, wounding two and murdering another, Renee Nicole Good. That lawlessness, that complete disregard for any norms, is both international and domestic policy with these two regimes. There are no limits, except my morality, Trump said yesterday to the *New York Times*.[1] Well, he has no morality. He's a convicted felon. He's a convicted sexual predator. He's a thief. And that absence of morality dictates that he can do anything he wants. The same applies to Netanyahu.

TA: And the Europeans just sit idly by. With the exception of Spain and partially Ireland, they have abandoned any notion of fighting back, even behind the scenes. There's a now-iconic photograph from Trump's visit in June 2025 in which Trump's papers have fallen to the ground and Keir Starmer, the British prime minister, is literally on his knees at Trump's feet, picking them up for him. It's the most symbolic photograph of Europe vis-à-vis the United States today. Whereas immediately after the Second World War, there were political figures who looked upon US power critically and with great skepticism: Adenauer criticized the Americans behind the scenes; de Gaulle was public in his criticisms and was opposed to extending EU membership to countries that were total US stooges. That's all gone. These are sort of third-rate politicians who only seem second-rate when compared to Trump. Otherwise they are a disaster story. One would hope the Chinese might interfere to at least slow the US–Israeli advances, but they have their own interests. They sometimes speak quite strongly, but they do little, if anything, to undermine the US in a materially effective way. Why has China been reluctant to break off relations, diplomatic or trade, with Israel?

RK: They do have very important connections to Israel in terms of security and arms. China was the third largest importer of Israeli goods in 2024 and the biggest exporter of goods to Israel, so there is a significant trade relationship there.[2] On top of that, before October 7, Israel was China's second largest supplier of military technology and defense systems. For reasons that have much more to do with conflicting strategic interests than solidarity with Palestine, China and Israel's trade relationship regarding defense-related materials has shifted since October 2023. But China controls 80 percent of the global drone market and has an incentive to sell its product. Israel has reportedly used thousands of Chinese-manufactured drones to do reconnaissance over and carry bombs to Gaza. That said, Israel barely made it into the top fifty list of countries importing goods from China in 2025, so ending or at least limiting trade relations would have cost China a little bit, but not very much.

TA: Not too much. The same could be said of this Sultan of Donkeys, as I call him, Erdoğan, in Turkey. Just six months ago, in July 2025, Turkey made big noise calling for an embargo on arms trade to Israel, but Turkish ports have continued to be a central hub for arms being shipped to and from Israel. Just the other day, Turkish activists wrote that Turkish trading vessels were being unloaded with materiel for Israel, including weapons. Turkish arms exports are expanding rapidly. The first half of 2025 saw a 25 percent increase in defense exports from Turkey relative to the previous year. Turkey is, of course, not alone. The global arms industry is growing very quickly and everyone wants a piece of the pie. Still, the US remains dominant, and Israel is backed by the US completely.

RK: We're not in a multipolar world. It appears that we are, in some respects, moving toward that, but we're not yet in a multipolar world. The US military remains absolutely singular in its dominance and global reach. It's also crucial to remember that Trump is a bully and people are afraid of him. Even in his own party. Only Marjorie Taylor Greene and a few dissidents—mainly women, incidentally, like Nancy Mace, women whose politics are abhorrent to most of us—have had the courage to say, "This man is a bully." Marjorie Taylor Greene herself just resigned from Congress a couple of days ago, allegedly because Trump was bullying her to fall into line, to adopt his policies and program, and she saw no point in continuing. Ultimately, I think that's true as well of your European dwarves who populate the prime ministerships and the chancellorships of the various European countries. These people are really afraid of him.

TA: Okay, let's move on to even more depressing matters.

[*Laughter from TA and RK*]

RK: If that were possible.

TA: Let's look at the balance sheet of what has been happening in the Middle East, particularly, of course, in

Gaza and the West Bank, since October 7. Most of Gaza is occupied. The West Bank is under siege every day by Zionist fanatics of one sort or the other, backed by the IDF. We've seen the targeted murders of political leaders across the region: in the case of Yemen, the entire cabinet; in Lebanon, the pager attack on many Hezbollah activists and the execution of their leader, Hassan Nasrallah; and of course the assassination of Hamas's leader, Yahya al-Sinwar. Syria is now occupied after a joint Israeli-Turkish intervention. On this last point, what many people don't understand fully is that with the capture of Syria, the last remnants of a specific sort of Arab nationalism is gone. Iraq, Egypt, Syria, every single one of these states, regardless of the quality of their leaders—Saddam Hussein, Hafez al-Assad, Bashar al-Assad, Muammar Gaddafi—asserted and defended their sovereignty on the foundation of Arab nationalism, albeit bad manifestations of it. Now that's all gone. So there is a way in which one could argue that in addition to the dismemberment of Gaza and the genocidal killings, Israel has emerged as a power which is of even more importance to the United States because of its strategic capacity to wipe out entire layers of political leaderships and redraw regional power structures.

RK: That's a grim picture, but I think it's essentially accurate. I would only add to it the following. You correctly pointed to the demolition of these strong states created by these dictatorial regimes. But what has taken the place of a number of them are divided, failed states, collapsed states, non-states, no states. There's no real state in the Sudan. There's no real state in Yemen. There's no real state in Libya. There's no state in Syria. There are the shambles and the simulacrum in some places of a central authority, which controls a fraction of the territory, as is the case in Iraq. So the countries that had these powerful regimes have been demolished one by one, in some cases by direct American intervention, Iraq being the model example, in some cases by multiple interventions, as with Syria and Libya, and in some cases by internecine domestic conflict combined with proxy wars by regional powers: the Emirates and Saudi Arabia, for example, as well as the United States, France, and Britain. In Libya, the French support Khalifa Haftar's Libyan National Army and the British support the Government of National Accord, led by Fayez al-Serraj. The Egyptians are on one side while the Turks and the Emiratis are on another side with the Israelis. That's the status of six or seven Arab countries that formerly were unified—dictatorial, undemocratic, oppressive, but unified. Some of these states were relatively powerful and had, as you suggested, a measure of sovereignty. Who is sovereign in Syria? Who is sovereign in Yemen? Who is sovereign in the Sudan? There's no sovereign. There are multiple external powers and multiple internal factions.

This is a state to which both the decay and collapse of that Arab nationalist formula and constant external intervention have contributed. Israel, too, has played a role in this, but think back to Kissinger and his passionate commitment to weakening these states that were an obstacle to the United States, whether by separating them from the Soviet Union during the Cold War, or by bringing them into an alliance on a basis of inferiority to Israel, as he helped to do with Egypt in the 1970s. The Camp David Accords turned Egypt into a vassal state of the US and Israel. All of this has contributed to the situation in Palestine, of course. Where are the Arab countries? Well, they're run by regimes that are afraid of their own people—if there even is a single regime. In Algeria, Saudi Arabia, and the UAE, for instance, you have a unified regime, but they have almost no domestic legitimacy except through the bribes they pay their citizens through oil rent, which is distributed unequally to the population. The Gulf countries and some others are dependent for their internal and external security on the United States, and in the case of the Emirates, to a certain extent, on Israel. The Emirates' antimissile defenses were built and are controlled by Raytheon Israel. So even these countries—Algeria, Egypt, Saudi Arabia, the UAE, and so on—are not fully sovereign.

The support for the Palestinians that is pretty much a constant feature of public opinion in these Arab countries has no way of expressing itself in the face of these repressive dictatorial regimes. Where a regime even exists. And for the other countries, how can you ask Iraqis, who still do not have electricity twenty-four hours a day, twenty-two years after the American invasion destroyed their oil industry and their electrical grid, to revolt and demonstrate for Palestine? This is one of the largest producers of oil in the world. This is a country with unlimited energy. They don't have electricity, and the country is divided under malicious, corrupt militias, and a central government that is one of the greatest instances of kleptocracy in world history. How do you expect Syrians? How do you expect Yemenis? How do you expect people who are living in a situation of almost constant civil war and external intervention—Sudanese, Libyans, Lebanese—to pay attention to Palestine? I mean, they have to run their generators or work on solar power to even have internet or have their fridges run. People are being worn down in these countries by the dissolution of the state. I'm no great fan of the state, but having a state, particularly one with some legal norms, is certainly better than a situation of complete chaos and illegality.

TA: Let's turn to Lebanon, since it's been quite an important entity—let's put it like that—since it was created by the French after the First World War as a little slither off the coast to protect French interests. What is the state of Hezbollah after Israel's assassination of its leadership, particularly the assassination of Nasrallah? What support is there for them?

RK: I haven't been to Lebanon in a while. I've been in other parts of the Middle East, I've been in Palestine recently, I've been in Turkey and Egypt recently, but I haven't been in Lebanon recently and it's sometimes hard to get a clear sense of what's going on without being there. The first thing to say is that Hezbollah has been measurably weakened. Its connection to Iran has been weakened, and Iran itself has been weakened. Besides the enormous domestic unrest, Iran's antiaircraft defenses, and much of its ballistic missile manufacturing capabilities, were destroyed by the Israelis and the Americans last July during the so-called Twelve-Day War. Some of its nuclear installations were also hit. We don't know the degree of the damage, but Iran is weaker and Hezbollah's connection to Iran via Iraq and Syria has been interrupted. So Hezbollah is an orphan in terms of external support. The Syrian regime, which it depended on and which it supported, is gone. Iraq is changing, as well. So, a movement that had what appeared to be powerful allies, what people called an "axis of resistance," has been stripped of much of its external support. Despite this, it has carried on fighting and has scored some serious hits against the IDF.

In addition, there's a lot of questioning inside Lebanon, by Lebanese generally, and even I would argue among some Shi'a, about the strategy followed by Hezbollah. I personally think that Hamas drew Hezbollah into a conflict that Hezbollah was not prepared for and was not warned about and was not ready for. Hezbollah's military strength was built up with Iranian support, essentially in order to provide deterrence against Israel attacking Lebanon or attacking Iran—from the Iranian perspective, mainly to prevent Israel from attacking Iran. "If you attack us, you will face a rain of tens of thousands of projectiles from Lebanon." That was a deterrent. And anyone who knows anything about deterrence theory knows that when it becomes necessary to use a deterrent, it has failed. So, that whole military structure was not constructed to fight a year-and-a-half war of attrition against Israel. It was constructed as a deterrent to prevent Israel from attacking both Lebanon and Iran.

When Hamas launched this operation on October 7, 2023, it put Hezbollah in an impossible position. If it didn't act, it was failing to support its Arab brethren and its stated commitment to Palestine would seem hollow. Iran was put in a similarly difficult position. Both fell into what I would argue was a trap. It wasn't a trap laid by Israel. Hamas assumed, I think falsely, that everybody would just fall in line when they lit the spark. Everyone who made the key decisions was inside Gaza and they're all dead now, as far as we know, so we can't know exactly what their calculation was. The Israelis claim to have collected documents, but I wouldn't believe anything the Israelis publish. One day we may see those documents and be able to test them but that day may be far away. The point is, whatever Hamas intended, the result as far as Hezbollah is concerned was that it was drawn into a conflict it couldn't possibly win. And Lebanon has been paying for this since the day after October 7, when Hezbollah started launching its rockets against northern Israel and other parts of Israel. So it is much weaker, which has changed the balance of forces inside Lebanon. The other Shi'a group, Amal, has become somewhat more powerful, and is headed by the eternal Speaker of the Lebanese Parliament, Nabih Berri. This war has emboldened all of Hezbollah's opponents inside Lebanon, who never really signed on to the ideas that motivate Hezbollah, whether they are Muslims or Christians or Druze.

Now, two other things have to be added. The United States and Israel are operating in tandem. The United States has allowed Israel to carry out this genocide and supported Israel in every measure, politically, militarily, etcetera. They bomb Lebanon every single day. They kill people in Lebanon every single day. They claim that they're going after Hezbollah operatives. They claim the Lebanese army isn't doing its job of trying to take over and disarm the south area, south of the Litani River. My sense is that the Lebanese Army has done some of the work that it claimed it was going to do in removing Hezbollah, militants and arms and tunnels and so forth, from the area south of the Litani. But Hezbollah still retains, I would assume, quite an arsenal in other parts of Lebanon. So you have a situation where America and Israel are pushing Lebanon toward what, if it is fully implemented, would possibly lead to a civil war because there are many people in Lebanon—in Hezbollah, among the Shi'a, and other supporters of Hezbollah outside of the Shi'a community—who say that Hezbollah cannot and should not give up its weapons until and unless Israel withdraws from occupied territory in South Lebanon, until and unless Israel ceases its constant attacks on Lebanon. So far, the Lebanese government has resisted these pressures, but they are overwhelming because the United States has made capitulation to its demands the condition for the rebuilding of Lebanon, for the release of the funds that are necessary to deal with the devastation that Israel has wreaked on this country over the past two years. They're therefore in an impossible situation in the Lebanese government, caught between the devil and the deep blue sea, the Israelis and the Americans on the one side, and the intransigence of Hezbollah on the other.

TA: You don't think they could just dismember the country quite openly, as they have done in other parts of the Arab world, giving different factions the chance to rule, as you described earlier in the cases of Libya and Iraq? Why couldn't they just let the Hezbollah people have their little bit of land in the south and take over the rest, like they're trying to do in the West Bank and Gaza? Though their aims are more open in the latter cases—they just want it all. Couldn't they do something like that?

RK: Well, Israel has that as an objective in Syria, for sure. It would like to divide Syria up into little statelets, at least two of which it would hope to bring under its control as protectorates, a Kurdish protectorate and a Druze protectorate. It already has laid the groundwork for a Druze protectorate, developing close relations with some Druze in the southern part of the country, as they have done with the Kurdish autonomous region in northern Iraq for many decades.

That is a possible Israeli objective in Lebanon. I

think, though, the Israelis want to completely destroy Hezbollah, including up to the point of forcing a new Lebanese civil war. I don't think they're willing to allow statelets that are hostile to them to even exist. Certainly not in such close proximity to Israel. Lebanon and Syria border on Israel. Having a hostile Sunni regime in Damascus seems to me to be something that the Israelis won't countenance. Their hostility to the new Syrian regime, which is supported by the United States, Saudi Arabia, and other Gulf countries, is one of the contradictions between the United States and Israel. The Americans are insistent on trying to rebuild a unified Syria under this regime, and the Israelis are insistent on keeping Syria divided. The Turks are part of that, as well, because they have their own sphere of influence in the north. So the redivision of Lebanon is something that the Lebanese are inoculated against. Remember, the Lebanese Civil War began in the 1970s. For most of the period of the civil war from 1975 to 1990, the Lebanese went through a division of their country along "the green line," which mainly separated Christians in East Beirut from Muslims in West Beirut. There's a very strong, atavistic sense among Lebanese that they do not want to be divided again. I don't know if that's enough to overcome the constant daily pressure of Israel, but if there is one mitigating factor, the memory of that period might be it. Also, I'm not sure the Americans want either Syria or Lebanon to be further divided. They're pushing very hard to prevent that in Syria. It surprises me a little bit, because they go along with the Israelis on so many other things. They've gone along with them completely insofar as pounding Lebanon is concerned. The same goes for the West Bank, Somaliland, and so many other Israeli initiatives. The US is backing the Israeli intervention, together with the Emirates, in Sudan and Libya. It's a veiled intervention. The Emirates are the cat's paw, and underneath it is clandestine Israeli involvement.

TA: Rashid, there's quite an astonishing little episode that took place a few weeks ago in which the Turkish foreign minister, Hakan Fidan, was visiting Damascus and gave a speech in the presence of [Abu Mohammed al-] Jolani, this al-Qaeda joker who the Americans and the Israelis have put into power. Just as Fidan started attacking Israel on Palestine and denouncing what the Israelis were doing, the Syrians switched off his mic.

[*Laughter from RK and TA*]

TA: So Fidan, the Turkish foreign minister, was on an official trip to Syria, but this Syrian regime cannot allow any criticism of Israel, so they switched off his mic.

RK: It would be unbelievable, but for the fact that just as Trump has extended this untrammeled expression of American power, Israel has expanded its power far beyond anything that it ever did before, even after occupying the territory of several Arab states in 1967. Its intervention, direct and indirect, covert and overt, in more than a half-dozen neighboring countries, is blatant and overt. They boast about it. You read Israeli strategists saying that they bestride the region like a colossus now. The apparent weakening of Iran has measurably increased Israel's power. The only other countries that have any weight in the region are Saudi Arabia, which is, in some ways, a paper tiger in that it doesn't have the capability to defend itself, and Turkey. Iran is a shadow of its former self.[3] Egypt is almost neutered in terms of its ability to project power.

TA: One of the long-term aims, of course, of the United States and the Israelis has been to neutralize Syria and Iran. When Baghdad fell in 2003, the Israeli ambassador to the United States publicly said, "Congratulations! Now let's finish the job by marching to Damascus and Tehran." Well, they've got Damascus.

RK: They may get Iran. I think it's touch and go in Iran right now.

TA: You think they will invade Iran?

RK: No, I think they'll try and bring down the regime. The Americans may attack. The Israelis *want* to attack. Reading the Israeli press this morning, it appears that the Americans are restraining them insofar as an attack on Iran is concerned, perhaps hoping either to weaken the regime and cut a deal or to bring the regime down. That seems to be the American calculation.

TA: The method is the same as they're using, of course, in Venezuela. Put a regime under debilitating sanctions, it can't satisfy the needs of its people, people get angry. Many comparisons have been made to the US invasion of Iraq in 2003. That was, of course, another US oil-seeking adventure that never realized the returns its architects promised. At the moment, it looks like the US oil barons aren't going to take Trump's bait in Venezuela, so he's already running into trouble on that score. Meanwhile, the *New York Times*, the day of Maduro's abduction, described the streets of Caracas as "chillingly silent" compared to those of Baghdad after Saddam Hussein's toppling in 2003. This suggests that despite Maduro's many flaws, ordinary Venezuelans, including many Maduro oppositionists, are opposed to a US intervention. I have a feeling that if a similar question were asked in Iran, the response would not be too different. There is absolutely no doubt that the internal opposition to the Iranian regime is, to a large extent, genuine. However, when I see demonstrators attacking hospitals and ambulances, and targeting the police, I do get a feeling that Iranian demonstrators would not damage their own social services in such a brutal way. This seems like a softening up of the country.[4]

RK: The other nasty element is that they're pushing the son of the Shah as a stooge to take over, and there are demonstrations in his favor now. Who is financing those demonstrations? Are they genuine?

TA: Well, I think it's without any doubt Israel, because the little Shah, just before the last upheaval in Tehran, went to Jerusalem to pose in photographs at the Wailing Wall. He's very open about his commitment to Israel. Less so to Iran.

RK: He's an Israeli stooge, there's no question. But the Iranians may be desperate because of the economic conditions that you mentioned. And this is not just Iran. This is Cuba. This is Venezuela. This is a number of countries that the United States wants to bring to their knees. It puts these sanctions on them and brings public opinion to its side, not because they like the Americans or want American intervention, but because they can't make ends meet because the economy has been collapsed by these sanctions, or by mismanagement and sanctions.

TA: The ultimate aim of all this, in my opinion, is to enable the US to tell China they will not get energy from the areas under US control without permission.

RK: Oh, yes.

TA: The US is effectively saying to China, "We will grant that permission in return for other goodies from you, but you will have to go through us. You can't deal directly with Iran, Venezuela, or other countries we don't like." This China obsession in the US is very strong. But let's say they topple the regime in Iran. They organize some pseudo-election, or a referendum, and this imbecilic son of the Shah is put on the Peacock Throne, so-called, and then what? That will not be a stable, medium-term solution.

RK: No, no, no. It's hard to predict any of these things, but whatever opposition there is to the regime in Tehran, there's a lot of support for the regime as well. One could say that the middle classes are dissatisfied and people are angry about the economic situation. But there is a core of support for the regime. If they try to bring the regime down, they're going to be met with a very powerful opposition, which is going to mean a great deal of instability. If the puppet Shah is installed, supported by the Israelis and the Americans, on the Peacock Throne, we're going to see a lot of unrest in many parts of Iran among supporters of the former regime. And maybe that's the objective. Again, the goal, at least for Israel, is to weaken Iran in the same way Iraq and Syria and Yemen and Libya and Sudan and Lebanon were weakened.

TA: That seems to be the imperial strategy now, because when asked not so long ago what the EU's plans for Russia are, the so-called EU Foreign Minister Kaja Kallas replied that they'd like to divide Russia up into smaller states so it doesn't pose a threat anymore. If that's the strategy they want to pursue, they'll come a cropper and could provoke a world war. Related to all this, the Israelis did something stupid, even from their own point of view, when they tried to kill the Hamas negotiators in Qatar. For the first time, the Saudis got really worried and flew in the Pakistani military chief, Asim Munir. None of this has come out, of course, since they fund Pakistan through free oil supplies. I think there's very little doubt, though some of my informants say we don't have the proof, that the Saudis said to Pakistan that if the US and Israel try to do something to us and bomb the holy places, we will need your weaponry and that this was promised.

RK: I believe that. The Saudis, the Egyptians, several other Gulf countries, were shocked by the attack on Qatar. It was a bridge too far. It changed the attitude of a number of Gulf countries to Israel, which had, mistakenly perhaps, overestimated the power of Iran, believing in this idea of the "axis of resistance," that Iran has proxies, Iran is so powerful, and so on. All of this American-Israeli hype was internalized by the colonized minds of the Gulf elites. Then suddenly they realized that Iran is a paper tiger, is extremely weak, and the Israelis are bombing us. These elites are all related to each other along the Gulf. They're all connected, these ruling families and the populations from Iraq down to Oman are deeply connected and they rightly feel that when you bomb Qatar, you're bombing us. And this is true of other governments that were in various ways favorably inclined toward Israel, or at least neutral toward Israel. They suddenly realized that Israel poses a danger to them. This untrammeled, aggressive behavior could be turned on any of them. If the Israelis can bomb the country with the largest American airbase in the

Gulf, and can then bomb Hamas negotiators dealing with an American peace plan, they can do anything.

I detected a shift in relation to Israel immediately after that episode, not just as you suggest in Saudi Arabia, which was the most important, but also in a number of other Arab countries. They became much more afraid of Israel, much more wary. In the case of Egypt, there were reports in the Egyptian media about the same time that Israel had plans to assassinate Hamas leaders involved in negotiations with Israel in Cairo. The fact that it was allowed to bubble up in the Egyptian media means that the regime was concerned. Whether it's true or not, that's not the point. The point is that they had the same concerns that the Saudis and the elites in the Gulf had after the attack on Qatar. I believe this was about the same time or maybe even before the attack on Qatar. So I think that event shifted things in relation to Israel.

The upshot is that there is now a much more cohesive position between these countries, and Turkey and Pakistan in trying to pressure the Americans in terms of Lebanon and of their dealings with Hamas and their dealings with Gaza. They have come back to talk to the Americans again and again about the failure of Israel to allow sufficient supplies in, about the shutting down of NGOs in the Gaza Strip, about various cruelties and horrors that Israel is inflicting on Gaza. They're doing it quietly. I don't think they're throwing their weight around as they should and could, but I think that's a change since the attack on Qatar. An understanding that maybe we had better stick together a little bit. Differences between Turkey and Egypt, differences between Saudi Arabia and Turkey, have been papered over in order to present something of a united front around Gaza and Lebanon to the Americans. So I agree with you. I think one of the worst mistakes Israel has ever made was its attack on Qatar. And even many Israeli commentators agree, by the way; this is not just you and me.

TA: The Qatar episode may have marked a shift in Arab states' positioning vis-à-vis the US and Israel, but as we've discussed, they have still by and large capitulated to US–Israeli aggression. There are, of course, important exceptions, particularly Algeria to a degree and the courageous Houthis in Yemen, whose entire cabinet leadership was wiped out by the Israelis.

RK: And their military commander was killed. There's no question of their courage. They were willing to endure punishment at an extraordinary level and did not stop until the so-called ceasefire. There was a report in a US naval publication about the extreme difficulty that the United States faced in its naval campaign in the Red Sea against the Houthis. It was framed in terms of lessons learned and the various difficulties they encountered, and what's obvious is that this is a tenacious, difficult foe. The Houthis' military prowess is clear from the number of planes that the United States lost. One F-18 Hornet was shot down because so many drones and missiles were being fired at US naval vessels that they had to send up planes to shoot some of them down. An American destroyer shot down one of their own planes in the melee. In another case, an aircraft carrier had to make a sharp turn to avoid being hit by Yemeni missiles and a plane fell off the side of the carrier. Another F-18 crashed as part of normal operations. So they lost three extremely expensive, sophisticated warplanes in this war with the Houthis. The Houthis not only showed courage, they showed enormous adaptability, according to this American naval assessment—this is not my opinion, this is what a US Navy analyst said. They closed the port of Eilat for the better part of two years; no ships could put in. They were hitting anything that went toward Eilat. And the Suez Canal was drastically affected, as well. Maersk, one of the biggest shipping companies in the world, resumed its shipments via the Suez Canal only two weeks ago after suspending them for over two years. Egypt lost a fortune because shipping was diverted as a result of this war. The Houthis had an enormous impact. That's what one tiny country can do. Or one faction in one tiny country! As a Yemeni friend of mine said, "Things would be different in Palestine if we were your neighbors."

TA: Absolutely true. When I went to Yemen some years ago, I spoke to many people, including the former leftists, who are now in the United Regime. One of them, the education minister, said to me, "Tariq, you must not underestimate that even though our leftist period in South

Yemen ended in disaster via shooting each other and all that horrible business, some of the reforms we pushed through in favor of women, in favor of peasants, left their mark. So we have helped to create a new consciousness." I conceded to him at the time that this was absolutely true for the South, but argued that they hadn't done that in the North, which was effectively controlled by the Saudis and the Egyptians. He said that the Houthis would learn. I must say that that old guy turned out to be right about what was happening in Yemen.

RK: The other thing to say about Yemen is that my understanding from people who are not supporters of the Houthis is that their position, and this is Yemenis in the United States and Yemenis in Yemen, their position toward Israel is supported across the board by other Yemenis. I know Yemenis who are at odds with the Houthis on various issues, but they completely support what the Houthis are doing regarding Israel. A particularly interesting development is that the Israeli–Emirati Southern Transitional Council, which purports to be in favor of reestablishing an independent South Yemen, has clearly miscalculated. Or rather, the Emirati–Israeli supporters of this group have clearly miscalculated, because the Saudis have reacted in an extraordinarily forceful way and have just completely cleared them out.

This Southern Transitional Council, according to a report today, was dissolved. Their leader fled to the Emirates, according to what the Saudis said, and the Saudi-backed forces have retaken the entire area of

South Yemen that these Emirati-backed folks had conquered in a lightning advance a couple of weeks ago. This looks like the beginning of a serious Emirati–Saudi conflict in Yemen. The Emiratis removed their troops, and when they did that, they removed the command-and-control structure for their proxies, who immediately folded as soon as the Emiratis left. This has implications for other areas where these powers are on opposite sides, for Libya, for Chad, for Sudan, for Somaliland, and possibly also for Palestine, Lebanon, and Syria. In each of these cases, the Emiratis are acting as stalking horses for Israel. Whether they have their own independent policy or there's mind control by the Israelis is not clear. But they have operated in close coordination with Israel in places like Somaliland, establishing bases for them in places like Socotra, which is part of Yemen.

The fact that the Saudis are reacting so strongly goes back to what I said earlier, that the attack on Qatar changed minds in Riyadh, in Cairo, and in a few other Arab capitals. This is a matter of Saudi security. These are areas that border on southern Saudi Arabia, areas that Saudi Arabia has always thought of as their sphere of influence, and they're not going to let the Emiratis mess with it because it's not just the Emiratis—where the Emiratis are, the Israelis are. I think the Saudis have realized that there's a threat to their national security here, not just from the Emirates, but actually from Israel.

TA: I think that is how it seems, Rashid. I'm just wondering, given that the Emiratis don't need to do this, given that they have enormous amounts of wealth in their country, why would they fall into the Israelis' laps in this way and debase themselves? One big reason could be that the Americans asked them to, saying, this is the key state in this area and, if you want to help us, you have to work with this state, and they capitulated.

RK: Either that or what we call now, in talking about American university administrations, anticipatory obedience. The idea is that the path to Washington runs through Tel Aviv, so we kiss the ring of whatever Israeli leader there is in order to gain the favor of Washington. That was the theory that Sadat put forward decades ago. He actually said it: The path to Washington goes through Tel Aviv. That was his philosophy. So, whether the Americans are telling them to do this, or whether they believe this to be the case, it has the same impact. The other thing to say is that this may be just like what we observe in Trump and Netanyahu: an inability to see the limits of power, as one can perceive in Trump's behavior toward Greenland, Canada, the Europeans, Venezuela, obviously, and in his threats against Colombia and Mexico, and Israel's extension of its power all over the region. I think the same can be said about Mohamed bin Zayed, the Emirati ruler. Bin Zayed shares those delusions of grandeur, a sense that he can do anything, that he has unlimited power and can use it any way he wants, and Israel reinforces that. Israel gives the Emiratis the means to do things they couldn't do by themselves. So there's both a bit of megalomania, I would argue, in all three of these cases, and a misunderstanding of the limits to their power—and, in this case, possibly encouragement by the Israelis.

TA: In Qatar, of course, they've been slightly different in the sense that they have resisted intense pressure from the Americans, the Israelis, and the Saudis to close down Al Jazeera. This resistance now appears very surprising. I was in Qatar once and I asked the director running Al Jazeera, who was a sort of Hamas sympathizer, "Are you under any pressure?" He said, yes, all the time, but not from our government. He then told me a story that took place during the Iraq War. He said that their camera people caught sight of American Marines pilots targeting a car in which an Iraqi family was driving. That it was a family was obvious as there were two children in the back of the car. The marines made a joke of it and said, should we try and take them out? They then killed the family. The Al Jazeera crew caught it all. The footage arrived in the evening and the next morning they played it every hour on their news show. At five o'clock that afternoon, before their six o'clock news, the security guards at the station came running in and warned that the Americans were coming from the Al Udeid Air Base. The general walked into the director's office, reprimanded him for replaying this footage all day long, and demanded that he take it off the air. What this story revealed to me is that the Americans don't feel they need to go through the Qatari government. They think they run the country.

RK: On the one hand, Qatar shares its enormous gas field with Iran. They have to remain on a certain level of good relations with Iran because they share this huge gas field at the bottom of the Gulf. On the other hand, they host the largest American base in the region and that's a balancing act that very few other countries in the region try to emulate, though the Turks do it. The Qataris also understand that their support of the Palestinians gives them a leg up with Arab public opinion, which is supportive of the Palestinians. So that gives Qatar another shield, as it were. They have a shield against Iran, a shield from the Americans, and a shield from Al Jazeera, and their policies of support for the Palestinians via Arab sentiment that is pro-Palestinian and which they cultivate. Now, this is a very dangerous game for a very small country. It got them into trouble with the Arab League from 2017 to 2021, when Saudi Arabia, the Emiratis, Bahrain, and Egypt all severed diplomatic ties with Qatar. The Saudis effectively imposed a blockade by closing the Abu Samra crossing, which is Qatar's only land crossing. Right now, the Saudis and the Qataris are on good terms, and Qatar is an invaluable partner in this alliance. They are trying to persuade the Americans to lift the siege of the Gaza Strip and to move to a phase of the so-called ceasefire where they actually *cease fire*, allow the rebuilding of Gaza, and where the Israelis finally withdraw from the majority of the Gaza Strip, which they still occupy. The Turks appreciate them for this, as do the Egyptians, though there's a rivalry between the Egyptians and the Qataris, both of which want to be the main interlocutor between the Americans, Hamas, and Israel. It's a delicate dance for them to engage in.

But it's a dangerous region—not just the Gulf, but the whole Middle East. It's worst, obviously, for regular people who don't have electricity, as is the case in Iraq or Gaza. Follow the meteorology in this region. It is raining a lot this winter. In Gaza, there are 900,000 people in tents that do not keep the rain out, that do not stand up to the wind. Of the 2.3 million people in Gaza, nearly half don't have proper shelter and the Israelis just will not let into Gaza the serious kinds of tents, or even better, mobile homes, which would provide temporary accommodation. All of these countries are feebly trying to do something about that while the Americans are, so far, just completely allowing the Israelis to get away with what, in effect, amounts to murder: the murder of children who die of hypothermia; the murder of people who become sick for no reason because they're soaking wet and cannot dry off; the murder of people who have wounds that will not heal; the murder of people who can't reach hospital because the crossing points are closed, and Oxfam and other NGOs have just been banned by Israel. So the limited health infrastructure that they support is being systematically undermined by this cruel, vicious, genocidal policy of preventing the reconstruction of anything in Gaza, but in particular, of the health infrastructure. It's an incredibly grim scenario.

TA: Rashid, we've been discussing the Arab world, of course, and the problems within it, as well as the sort of tiny places where there have been acts of solidarity, like Yemen. But one part of the world that has demonstrated a great deal of solidarity with the Palestinians is South America. When Operation Cast Lead took place in 2008–9, of which many journalists who write about Israel and Palestine display a staggering level of ignorance, Hugo Chávez, who was then the president of Venezuela, attacked it in the most aggressive language, broke off all diplomatic and trade relations with Israel, and kicked the Israeli ambassador out of the country. Soon after he did that, Evo Morales in Bolivia followed suit. The Chilean government, quite moderate by comparison, was also very pro-Palestine at the time.

RK: They have a very large Palestinian community in Chile.

TA: Indeed. When Chávez traveled to Qatar in the aughts, Al Jazeera recorded a one-and-a-half-hour-long interview with him. They then did something clever. They got one of the best Arab actors to do a dubbed translation, so it sounded to many as if he were speaking in Arabic. The guy who did the interview later told me that they had never received such a huge response from the Arab world. He said they had to hire six extra staff members to reply to all the letters and emails they got, so I asked what all these letters and emails said. He told me that 95 percent of the letters asked the same question in different ways: When will the Arab world produce a Chávez? So, this solidarity resonates among the Arab population, who can't help but compare it to their own wretched leaders, many of whom are on their knees to the United States.

More recently, Colombia's president, Gustavo Petro, was one of the earliest state leaders to describe Israel's actions in Gaza as a genocide. The contrast between the Arab leaders and the states they represent and Latin Americans thousands of miles away is jarring. When Maduro was kidnapped last week, Netanyahu was elated and couldn't resist saying that he applauded the US's "determined decision to restore freedom and justice" to Venezuela and, even more shamelessly, that South America is undergoing a political transformation that is leading several countries to "return to the American axis and, not surprisingly, also to a connection with the state of Israel." He was describing not only Venezuela, whose leader had just been brazenly abducted outside of all norms of international law, but also countries like Argentina and Chile, which have elected far-right candidates. He couldn't be more explicit about who his allies are.

RK: I mean, this is one of the tragedies of the Arab world. There are undemocratic regimes, or failed, collapsed, destroyed states, spread across most of this region, which prevents the expression of public opinion, which is supportive of the Palestinians. Instead, you have these weak-kneed, cowardly regimes dependent on the favor of the United States, or even on the favor of Israel. Even in the rest of the world, public opinion has shifted in favor of Palestine and has become harshly critical of Israel. This is true, as you just mentioned, all across Latin America. It's even true in the West, in the white settler colonies in Australia, and New Zealand, and in Canada. It's true in the United States. It's true in Europe. Public opinion has shifted. I think perhaps permanently—I don't know, one shouldn't predict—but I think what has been seen cannot be unseen.

People have realized that everything they thought was true about Israel, to the extent to which they knew anything, is false. They have seen the reality. They've seen genocide live-streamed, day in, day out, for two full years. I don't think people, young people especially, are going to forget that. They also have learned to distrust, to have contempt for, the legacy mainstream corporate media, which continues to lie to them about what is happening in Palestine every day. Instead they've come to trust the young Palestinians in Gaza who risk their lives to live-stream the genocide and show them what is really happening in Gaza, all while Israeli drones watch what they do and systematically kill Gazan journalists, over 240 of them. These young people have learned that most of what the BBC and CNN and the *New York Times* tell you is an Israeli fabrication. So it's not just Latin America. I think it's younger people in general—not just progressive people, but younger people across the political spectrum. You see this on the right in the United States. They watch the same videos everybody else watches and have been affected in exactly the same way as progressive youth and politically disengaged youth have been affected by what they have seen. There is intense pushback against Israel among the far right—the polls are unequivocal. Young people on the right have become critical of Israel in a way similar to that of young people on the left or in the center. It's remarkable, in my view.

TA: The only sign of hope really has come not from within the Arab world, but from the rest of the world, where solidarity has taken off in unexpected ways. It's symbolized by the mayoral victories of Zohran Mamdani in New York and Katie Wilson in Seattle. The mainstream of the Democratic Party, local and national media, and the Israel lobby targeted Mamdani relentlessly for his support of Palestine and accused him of being a commie, but the fact that he won the primary and then the election, sticking quite firmly to his positions on Palestine, speaks volumes. The DNC and the Democrat leadership, on the other hand, are behaving like they've always done.

RK: You're absolutely right about the Democratic Party leadership, which is an aged leadership that still believes in all of the myths that were peddled about Israel in the 1960s when they came to maturity. Look at Pelosi and

Schumer, who are invariably utterly committed to this Zionist mythology or beholden to donors or whatever the case may be. Remember, Harry Truman was a Democrat, the man who pushed through partition in 1947, John F. Kennedy and Lyndon Johnson, the people who gave Israel arms for the first time, were Democrats. The leadership of the Democratic Party has been the bastion of support for Zionism and Israel for a long time. The base of the party, by contrast, is now in a completely different place—not just the young people, but the base generally. We've seen this at work in various elections and primaries, including the mayoral primaries in New York and Seattle last year.

I think a change is underway because a lot of Democratic elected officials are at odds with their party leadership because their base will not support them in a primary if they take those positions. Officials like Rahm Emanuel and Gavin Newsom, the governor of California, who are stalwarts of the Democratic Party, have made statements saying that they will not take a penny from AIPAC. When did one ever hear any Democratic politician, or any American politician, for that matter, say those words? The old guard of the party is still committed to the beliefs they held when they were in their twenties and thirties, and they are steadfast in their determination to maintain the American–Israeli relationship, at least in its essential form. But the younger party careerists are feeling the popular pressure. A similar phenomenon is playing out in the Republican Party, where its leadership is facing a challenge from below. An Institute for Middle East Understanding (IMEU) and YouGov poll published in December 2025 showed that 51 percent of young Republicans are critical of Israel. In five or ten years, those people are going to be the majority of Republican voters. Things are changing at the base. They haven't yet changed at the top.

I always issue a caution when I begin to sound too optimistic, which is that public opinion had turned against the Vietnam War by 1968 or 1969, after the Tet Offensive. A majority of public opinion turned against Bush's war in Iraq within a year and a half of the launching of the war. Bush invaded Iraq in March 2003. By the fall of 2004 public opinion had turned against the war in Iraq. And yet those wars continued for many, many years after public opinion shifted. So even if this shift is permanent, even if it continues to develop and grow, the opposition to war and opposition to this special relationship with Israel will likely take a long time to have any material effect on the people operating at the highest levels.

TA: In Britain, as I'm sure you've heard, a group called Palestine Action, who have been targeting Israeli factories in direct actions with great success and no violence, have been declared terrorists by the government and locked up. A number of those political prisoners are on hunger strike as you and I speak, and the media has warned that today could be the last day in the lives of two young hunger strikers. It would be a huge tragedy if they died, but it shows the intensity of feeling that Palestine is inspiring. The interesting thing is that old people, white people, British citizens, largely above the pensionable age, have come out in their hundreds all over the country to protest Palestine Action's proscription. They've organized mass sit-ins in which they simply carry signs that say, "I oppose genocide. I support Palestine Action," which the British police are compelled to treat as an act of terrorism. This has led to repeatedly broken records for the largest number of arrests made in a single day for decades. Ninety-year-olds being dragged off by an embarrassed British police force creates a shocking spectacle. But this shameless, appalling government has shown no intention to draw back so far.

RK: Two things: I think both the Irish and Indian examples show the absolute power of the hunger strike. It's an appalling thing when you think of it, killing yourself in order to prove a point. It shows a high degree of moral passion, obviously; it's an extraordinarily powerful tactic. In Cork there's a huge portrait of Mayor Terence MacSwiney, the Lord Mayor of Cork, who starved himself to death during a hunger strike in Brixton Prison in 1920. It's now 2026, and he's still an icon. It had an impact on British imperialism, both in Ireland and in India, this moral outrage represented by hunger strikes. It shows, as you said, that it's not just young people, though they're the main driver. They were the main driver of Mamdani's victory and the main driver of the change we've seen in American public opinion. The campuses played an instrumental role in instigating that shift. But I think it's gone to another level. This betokens a conflict with an elite that will not cease its blind support for Israel. They double down in the universities, in the media, in art galleries, in theaters. They will not allow Palestinian plays to be shown. They militate against Palestinian artists. They publish the same drivel by people like David Halbfinger, who basically adopted the role of stenographer for the Israelis in a piece that I just read yesterday, repeating Israeli claims paragraph after paragraph. These people have no credibility with ordinary, intelligent people who know what is actually happening in Gaza. They are losing the narrative, and they will not shift. We see it on US campuses, especially. Amazing things are happening on American campuses, where the pressure on students and the pressure on faculty is unceasing. However, I do not think that that position is going to be able to hold. Public opinion is too strong on this issue. People are going to see this in the American midterm elections, and it will likely harm the Labour government sooner or later.

TA: Despite this remarkable shift we're seeing toward popular support for Palestine, we must be honest that this period since October 7 has been a terrible defeat. We've lost Gaza. The West Bank is slowly being taken over by crooks. Trump's family wants to build apartments on the coast in Gaza, to transform it into a grotesque "Riviera of the Middle East." What do you think the future is for people in Palestine?

RK: I just came back from Palestine, where I was able to travel only in a very limited fashion around the West Bank, Jerusalem, Haifa, parts of the Galilee, and Jericho. I came away with the distinct impression that the horrific campaign in the West Bank has not forced Palestinians to leave Palestine. The Israelis are not going to be able to uproot them. They can try to drive people out of this or that community. They can burn homes, they burn cars, they can bulldoze refugee camps in Jenin and Tulkarm, and cut down olive trees. They can imprison people. There are 900 checkpoints in the West Bank. There are hundreds of barriers, these new red-and-yellow metal barriers that close off villages completely. None of this is going to drive the people off the land. You go to Galilee and you see what were once Arab villages, Palestinian villages, which are now medium-sized and small cities of 150,000 to 200,000 people. And although Israel has unleashed a crime wave against them, although the number of murders has gone above 300 per year in the Arab sector, the Palestinian sector inside Israel, the people are not going anywhere. They have failed to do what Herzl said: "We will spirit the penniless population across the frontiers." Didn't work. They expelled three-quarters of a million in 1948. They expelled 300,000 in 1967. And you still have an Arab majority in Palestine in 2026. And there are West Bank villages clinging to the land, even as the settlement project metastasizes all around them, even as the Israeli army and these thugs attack and attack and attack. For all the suffering—what has happened in Gaza is unspeakable—the people haven't left.

One could argue that they weren't allowed to leave. But had they demanded to leave, could the Egyptians and the other Arab states refuse to let them? They didn't demand to leave. They keep saying, we want to stay. That's true in the West Bank and it's true in Galilee. So from that point of view, this *sumud*, this steadfastness of the Palestinians on their land, has ultimately shown that the Zionist project has overreached. Without cataclysmic ethnic cleansing, which I hope they cannot—will not be allowed to—carry out, it cannot succeed.

There is a Palestinian people that will not be removed from Palestine, and that reality is becoming more clearly understood all over the world. In Latin America, as you said, but especially in the metropole. Without the metropole, Israel doesn't exist. Every Merkava tank, every Namer armored personnel carrier, operates with a German or American engine. Every warplane is American. Every combat helicopter is American. The Security Council vetoes are American. If they don't have those things, they can't wage their wars and they can't uproot Palestinian villagers. What Israel is doing would be impossible without the support of the metropole. And though the elites are scrambling to keep that support solid, it's eroding at the base. You're going to see this in elections sooner or later. We're already beginning to see it in the United States. Public opinion has shifted, and I think this is a change that we haven't seen since the days of Balfour and Woodrow Wilson.

There has always been support for Zionism in the West, whether caused by antisemitism, philosemitism, Christian Zionism, geopolitical strategy, Realpolitik. The governments are still with the Israelis, but public opinion is no longer, and the Palestinians are still holding fast to their land.

TA: This is of course extremely important. Let's just discuss briefly the so-called Palestinian Authority, which has no authority whatsoever. As we discussed in our last conversation, it's run by the IDF and the old PLO leadership led by Mahmoud Abbas. Abbas made one appearance at the height of the genocide, where he said that Hamas should hand over its weapons to the Palestinian Authority, and we never saw his creepy face again. Not to support your people, not to unite them, at the height of a genocide is just shocking. Now, over two years into this awful period, can the PA make any legitimate claim to represent the Palestinian people?

RK: No, they don't represent their people. They represent the people who pay them, which are mainly the people who give them orders: the Israelis, the Americans, and the Europeans. They are a cat's paw for foreign interests. They are not a national body, as they claim to be. This is a body that no longer represents, if it ever did, the Palestinian people. Arafat, in fact, once did represent the Palestinian people. There was lots of opposition to what he was doing, but he represented a majority. These people now represent a tiny minority.

The day when the Palestinians can actually choose their leadership and not be stuck with people imposed on them, as these folks are, will be a good day. There must be a revived national movement that represents the wishes of the Palestinian people. It's not clear what the Palestinians want, but you can only find that out once you've had a democratic transition, which is sorely needed, and which is something these people in the Palestinian Authority are terrified of having. They know that they would be voted out in a free and fair election.

As far as Hamas is concerned, they represent a strong tendency among the Palestinian public, but they never actually had a majority. In the 2006 election, they won 44 percent of the vote. They didn't win a majority. They won a majority of *seats* because of the way in which the districts were configured and because Fatah was split. It's like a British election, where a party can get only 33 percent of the vote and end up with a huge parliamentary majority because of first-past-the-post. They represent the idea of resistance. Most Palestinians ascribe to various forms of resistance, not only armed resistance. The Palestinians perform resistance simply by staying where they are. That's the most potent form of resistance that Palestinians can offer. There are many unwise forms of resistance. This is something that I've argued again and again. Resistance in and of itself is not sacred, or rather specific means of resistance are not sacred. There are strategic means, and there are less strategic means. There are intelligent means, and there are less intelligent means. There are means of resistance that are appropriate to a certain phase that may be inappropriate in another phase.

I am personally of the opinion that attacks on civilians are extremely unwise. Now, can you stop them completely? No. Did the Algerian FLN stop them? No. Did the IRA stop them? No. Did the ANC stop them? No. But they ended up forming governments. The government of Northern Ireland is now run by Sinn Féin. The government of South Africa is now run by the ANC. The government of Algeria—dictatorial and nondemocratic though it may be—is the descendant of the FLN. These people shot their way to power in ways some of which I find abhorrent. Nevertheless, I think that it can be argued that resistance, including armed resistance, to occupation and colonization is, first of all, legitimate, and secondly, necessary, but it has to be intelligent. It has to be strategic. It has to win you support. I have critiques of what Hamas did, among many other reasons, for this reason. I don't think it was strategic in many respects. Assuming that their allies would follow their lead without ever consulting them was not a strategic decision. Attacking Israeli civilians: How can that be justified? Hezbollah avoided that to a very large extent when it liberated South Lebanon in 2000. Many hundreds of people had collaborated with the Israelis. They didn't touch a hair on the head of one of them. That was a strategic, intelligent form of resistance. I know it's easy sitting in New York to talk about how purely you have to operate. I understand that it's much more difficult when you're on the ground, but still, I think that those general rules should be understood by anyone who supports Palestine, especially young people.

TA: I agree with you entirely on this, totally. It makes me think of that scene in *The Battle of Algiers* where the captured guerrilla leader is asked why the FLN blows up cafes when anyone can be injured or killed. He replies, "We don't have an air force, give us an air force and we would attack them from the air." It's the answer the Vietnamese used to give, as well. But the fact is that we do not have at the moment what the Vietnamese and the Algerian FLN had—a popular government, even in exile. All attempts to establish one have been muffled. Why do you think that is, Rashid?

RK: Well, two things. First of all, the word you just used, "exile." What national liberation movement sleepwalks into a cage controlled by the occupying power? Brings the entire movement inside the occupied territory? Just because you signed a deal with the people who've been destroying your country and your population for sixty years does not mean that you've liberated anything. Arafat and the PLO leadership made a terrible mistake in signing the Oslo Accords. The IRA had a base in the United States and in the UK and all over the world. It had people inside Ireland, but it kept part of the leadership outside. So did the FLN, the ANC, and the Vietnamese, because it's impossible to liberate your country from inside a prison controlled by the occupier.

Second, there's been a great deal of intervention to prevent elections. PA elections were held back in the early 2000s, during a period when Arafat and then Abbas were democratically elected as president. Then there was a democratic election which produced a parliament in 2006. There hasn't been an election since. Now, this is partially the result of people clinging to their chairs, but mostly it is Israel and the United States not wanting a democratic election because they fear it would return a result that they're not happy with, and would legitimate the Palestinian leadership that emerged. So there is an undemocratic tendency inside parts of the Palestinian polity, which is exacerbated by a desire to avoid democracy among the two powers that have the most control: the United States and Israel. Not to speak of the fact that the Arab countries don't want democracy for the Palestinians because most of them don't have democracy themselves, and in fact have been engaged in fighting democracy for their entire existences. The Saudis and the Emiratis put enormous effort into overturning the results of the Arab revolutions of 2011–12, and to ensure that tin-pot dictators and autocrats were put in place of the democratic regimes that otherwise might have developed in Tunisia, Egypt, Yemen, and Syria. So there are multiple forces that are preventing this, internal and external.

TA: Let's just return for a few minutes to what happened on October 7, now some two years ago. The debate about what actually happened carries on. It's very difficult to read a single document which gives an accurate account of what happened. Civilians were killed, there's no doubt. We know that. Many of the Israeli assertions regarding what happened that day—dozens of beheaded babies, and so on—were repeated and published by the mainstream press in the West only to be quietly disproven months later. The *New York Times* has been a particularly egregious offender on this score. What can we say with confidence happened on that day?

RK: Well, several things. First, whatever Hamas said they did or didn't do, they certainly gave orders to kill. I've seen video footage that appears to be of Mohammed Deif giving an order the morning of the attack to kill, so that they wantonly killed civilians seems unquestionable, whatever they say. Second, they had absolutely no control over this battlefield. Once the dozen or more breaches had been made in the fence, hordes of people poured across.

TA: People who were not under Hamas's control.

RK: No, just ordinary people. If you go back and look at videos from that morning, you'll see people on motorbikes carrying looted stuff or people they've captured, Israeli civilians, that they as individuals had captured. This is not Islamic Jihad, and it's not Hamas. It's the populace of the areas close to the fence that poured across. So were there killings of civilians? Of course there were. Some of them, I think, ordered by Hamas, as far as I can tell, but many of them possibly carried out by the people who surged across the frontier.

The second factor is the Hannibal Directive, Israel's use of air power to prevent people going back into Gaza, which included attacks on vehicles which had Israeli citizens aboard, who had been captured and had been taken hostage—both citizens and soldiers. The third thing is that we know that about 800 Israeli civilians were killed, many of them at the Nova music festival, others in the settlements along the border. Still others were probably killed by Israeli troops attacking the settlements that had been taken by Hamas, or attacking the vehicles that were taking people back into Gaza. Israel had no command and control that day. The Gaza division had been overrun. You read the Israeli accounts, which are now coming out, settlement by settlement, unit by unit, in the Israeli press and it's perfectly clear that the response was utterly chaotic. They did not take control of the areas that had been captured by Hamas for almost seventy-two hours. And in that period, there was no centralized control. Helicopters were ordered to just attack. Forces were put together by individual Israeli commanders who just grabbed whichever soldiers or policemen were nearby and willing to go to the battlefield. So some Israeli civilians were killed undoubtedly by Hamas and some were killed undoubtedly by Palestinians in Gaza who just poured out across the fence. But a lot of people were killed by the Israelis as part of their uncontrolled response.

The last thing is there were about 400 Israeli

soldiers and security personnel who were killed, and 800 civilians. The total Israeli death toll on that day and the day after was about 1,200, according to *Haaretz* and Israeli officials, of whom almost 400 were security personnel, mainly soldiers. So there was a huge battle. And in that battle, a lot of civilians were killed. And I'm sure others were wantonly killed because nobody controlled the battlefield. Beyond that, we don't know because Netanyahu's government will not allow an Israeli commission of inquiry, despite the fact that a lot of Israelis want to know what happened and with good reason. If I were an Israeli citizen, I would want to know what the hell happened. How was it that that 1,200 Israelis died that day? They simply haven't accounted for the fact that Israel was carrying out quite savage attacks on anybody who tried to cross back into Gaza. They must have killed a lot of their own civilians. There are also videos of rows of cars destroyed. What weapons did Hamas have to destroy dozens and dozens of vehicles? They had RPGs. They're not going to use an RPG on eighty cars in a row. That's clearly Israeli air power. Now, were people in those cars? I don't know. I think that situation will remain murky for a very long time. One day, we may know more than we know now. But if we just read the accounts that have been published, it's very hard to say. And we don't have accounts from Hamas. Most of the people engaged in that operation from the Palestinian side are dead. They've been killed in the subsequent war. We have Israeli accounts. We don't have journalists' reports because Israel has not allowed journalists into Gaza. So it's going to be very hard to find out the exact truth.

TA: Rashid, what about internal life in Israel itself? I mean, we have the figures, of course, no one denies it, that people might hate Netanyahu personally, but the Jewish Israeli population overwhelmingly supports the war. And that means that there is very little real opposition inside Israel itself, except a handful of very decent people, many of whom we know. In the old days, we used to say that possibly we would get some opposition inside Israel itself and unite with the Palestinians. They could create a decent state, but that looks a very long way away, if possible at all.

RK: It does look a long way away. I don't think that any solution is on the horizon. And I think that a change inside Israel will possibly have to wait for the change in Western public opinion to filter up to the hardened elites whose minds will not change right now. There have been, in the past, changes in Israeli public opinion as a result of shifts outside the country on a much more limited basis than what's needed now. Israelis have to accept that there's another people living there. Israel has shifted so far to the right that the Israeli Knesset voted in 2018 for a nation-state law declaring Israel the nation-state of the Jewish people, effectively denying that the Palestinians even exist. If you don't accept that there's another people there, how are you going to live with them? The answer, of course, is that they don't intend to live with them. They hope to either drive them out or make them so miserable and subjugate them to such a degree that they can be ignored. That's obviously not working. It cannot work. It involves a degree of fantasy that's spectacularly foolish. I don't know what external pressures will bring about a change in Israeli public opinion. As you already mentioned, the people who were the closest to understanding this are the ones who are leaving for Europe, for the United States, and for elsewhere.

I'm not sure how Israeli public opinion can be changed. October 7 was a terrible shock. It didn't create new views, it hardened views. A certain kind of callousness, a certain kind of racism, a certain kind of complete disregard for Arab life, which was always there, was enormously enhanced by the trauma of what happened. Israelis assumed that they were safe and that any damage to Israel or to them would be limited. What happened on October 7 shattered that illusion, and the anger and the bitterness and the chagrin has turned what was already a society quite hostile toward the Arabs into a society in which 60 or 70 percent of people support genocide. As you say, it is not a war. I gave a talk where I used as an example Marina Carr's play *Hecuba*, in which she talks about the fall of Troy and the queen says that this is not a war, this is genocide. But the Israelis refused to give up the charade, insisting that it's a just war and they will not accept the term "genocide." So it's going to take a lot to change Israeli opinion.

It's also going to take a lot to change Palestinian

opinion. After what's happened, most Palestinians don't believe, understandably, that there's any way they can live with Israelis. Even Palestinians inside Israel who grew up speaking Hebrew and have lived in Israel all of their lives are finding it harder and harder, given the intense racism and the discrimination and the political oppression to which they're subjected. And those are the people who are the best adapted to deal with Israeli realities. I spoke to a bunch of lawyers up in Haifa, and their account of the endless humiliation and harassment and callousness of Israeli Jewish society toward Palestinians makes it easy to see how very hard it is for them. It's infinitely hard for people in the West Bank, obviously, and it's unspeakable in Gaza, but they have a terribly difficult situation inside Israel because of the attitudes that have hardened to such a degree among Israelis after October 7. That will take time to ebb, if it ebbs at all. I think external shocks, external pressure, a realization that Israel can't go on as it has for the past several years, that it will no longer have support, that you're not going to get your tank engines from Germany and you're not going to get your F-35s from the United States, you're not going to get your vetoes in the Security Council if you keep up with this—that is the only way anything will change. That may not be tomorrow, it may not be in 2028, but it will come, I think. I hope.

TA: Rashid, I think you're right to end on a somewhat hopeful note. As we've discussed throughout this conversation, the Arab populations feel that their states have let the Palestinians down, and they're slightly ashamed that they were scared, that they haven't come out in the force they should have. This was the case in Pakistan after Zulfiqar Ali Bhutto was hanged by the military in 1979. The army was expecting an uprising, but nothing happened. And General Zia-ul-Haq, the dictator who massacred Palestinians in Black September in 1970 on behalf of the Jordanian government, said, triumphantly, "Not a bird twittered." Ten years later, the masses came out for Bhutto's daughter, Benazir, and one of the slogans I saw with my own eyes, at a demonstration of two million people, was "Benazir, forgive us, we kept quiet for your father." It makes me think of the Arab masses in relation to Palestine today. This anger could come out in other ways which neither you, nor I, nor anyone can predict.

RK: We shall see.

3.

May 1, 2026

Tariq Ali: Greetings, Rashid. We ended our last conversation speculating on what might or might not happen in the Arab world after the so-called ceasefire. In a utopian vein, I was suggesting that perhaps there would be a mass uprising of the Arab peoples that would change the situation. You were skeptical and said, "We shall see." In fact, what has happened is what neither of us predicted: a completely unprovoked war by the United States and Israel on Iran, and the bombing of Beirut with the IDF occupying southern Lebanon yet again. Trump, it's now clear, imagined that he could repeat the January operation in Venezuela, that they would have collaborators in the Iranian regime that would facilitate a managed transition of power to an Iranian leadership that would effectively do the Americans' bidding. He said in one of his tweets that "I'm going to choose who rules Iran [no question of democratic elections] like I chose Delcy in Venezuela." Trump pronounced this openly, no shame at all. Trump and his administration obviously didn't realize that the mood in Iran might change drastically, and in the Shi'a lands everywhere, after they killed Ali Khamenei, his wife, and much of their family. Khamenei's successor, his son Mojtaba Khamenei, is said to have been badly wounded. This execution of the country's principal leader created, even in a country like Pakistan, huge pro-Iran demonstrations, the likes of which I don't think either of us would have predicted. The other big surprise, certainly to me, was the speed with which, after Khamenei's killing, the Iranian regime decided to defend their sovereignty and fight back fiercely. And lots of people were amazed. Some were very pleased that Israel was getting a blasting and that Iran was bombing American bases in the Gulf states. All of this has shifted the balance of forces in the region. When we spoke in January, you said that Iran had been revealed as a "paper tiger" that is "extremely weak" after the US–Israeli attacks last June. Were you surprised by the Iranian fightback against this new wave of aggression?

Rashid Khalidi: I was wrong in January. This is a country that went through eight years of war with Iraq, during the course of which at least half a million people died. Iraq was supported at that time by almost every Arab country, by the Soviet Union, and by the United States and Western Europe. In that period, the Iraqis got their poison gas from the Germans (from the same firm that had made Zyklon B during the Second World War), they got their fighter planes from the Soviets, they got satellite reconnaissance from the Americans, they got collaboration from everybody on Earth. And these people fought for eight years and never gave up. And it was apparently only with the greatest difficulty that Ayatollah Khomeini was persuaded to stop the war. So, on reflection, in light of this, I wasn't surprised when they fought back so effectively, actually.

TA: In the Iran–Iraq War, though, there was a big debate within the clerical regime in Iran as to whether they should have stopped after they had taken back all their land. Khomeini resisted, but many clerics said, "Let's stop now while we're winning." And they took the war further, which I think was a big mistake.

RK: I'm far from being an expert on the internal workings of the Iranian regime now or then, but it seems clear that it happened exactly as you said: Most of the other clerics were opposed to the continuation of the war, and it was Khomeini's absolute insistence that kept it going as long as it did. I think what we have now, apparently, is a much less influential, much less powerful, much less charismatic son of Khamenei and a much more powerful Revolutionary Guard, who seem to be running the show. This includes Mohammad Bagher Ghalibaf, the Speaker of the Iranian Parliament, who's a former general in the Revolutionary Guard and is on Israel's list of targets. So it's a different Iran, and probably, strange to say, a more militant Iran than under Khamenei or even under Khomeini back in the 1980s.

TA: I think there's very little doubt about that. On the flipside, the clashes in the United States between the Trump administration, on the one hand, and the Pentagon, on the other, suggest an astonishing amount of disagreement over this war at the highest levels. Several US generals have been sacked, dismissed, while other generals, a retired general, suggested publicly a few days ago that this is a disaster that shouldn't have happened. This has not happened before so early in any conflict, to my memory, Rashid. Neither Korea, nor Vietnam, nor even the Gulf War provoked such discord.

RK: Never, you're absolutely right. Never. Part of the reason is that this is an infinitely more stupid war than any of the stupid wars the United States has waged in Afghanistan, Iraq, and other parts of this region. A senior retired admiral recently said something to the effect of, "We've war-gamed it up and down and back and forth. We can't control the Strait of Hormuz. We knew that." So obviously, the professional opinion was that this isn't a great idea. And I have heard from serving army officers that they've war-gamed this. Their conclusion was that a war with Iran cannot be won by the United States under any circumstances up to and including the use of tactical nuclear weapons. And I believe that that's a correct assessment. So any professional who has any self-respect would at least have had reservations. And some of them have now, as we've heard, come out to say that, or have been fired for saying whatever they said.

TA: The other side of this, of course, is that in the past you had people within different administrations who basically supported their country, but were not shy about saying that they're making a huge mistake or saying, "How is this in any way in our real interests to knock out Iran just because the Israelis are asking us to?" And so we come back to the question, which we've seen in the genocide against Gaza and now against the West Bank, which is not on the same scale but is pretty vicious, of the United States being in total hock to the Israeli regime. How is that explicable?

RK: Again, when one talks about historic mistakes—you know, Napoleon or Hitler marching on Moscow—I'm not suggesting this is on the same level. But it's not just going to war with Iran, which would have been folly under any circumstances. It's allowing Israel to lead the United States by the nose into a foolish war, which is going to have a long-term, and I would say disastrous, effect on the remaining support for Israel in the United States. You've seen the polls: Over 50 percent of young Republicans have a negative view of Israel. And if you go to young Democrats, far higher percentages: Israel is more unpopular than it ever was. Previously, it was always popular. It is now extraordinarily unpopular among 60 percent of the American public, and leading the United States into a foolish, unwinnable war that is causing dramatic effects in terms of gas prices and inflation and so forth.

It's going to rebound on Israel and on the American–Israeli relationship in ways that we can't even foresee because we haven't seen the end of this. We don't know where this goes, but so far the negative effects are already clear regarding this conflict with Iran, particularly since, as the *New York Times* pointed out, Netanyahu came to the White House and in the Situation Room persuaded the president to go all in. All of Trump's advisors thought that was crazy. One of them said, "This is bullshit." This is in a recent report in the *New York Times* about two weeks ago, one that's very revealing. Everybody knows it. Israel led the United States into a catastrophic war.

TA: A crucial question is how this war might reshape relations between the US and its Arab allies in the region. A particularly striking feature of this war is the Iranian regime's decision to bomb US military bases, which was quite a daring move both militarily and politically. They had been warning the US and Israel, "Don't underestimate us," for some time and now they've made good on the warning. Knocking out the US bases in Kuwait, attacking the US base in Bahrain, threatening the Saudis, bombing the UAE and Qatar, all this has had an impact. It's divided these little Gulf states from each other. The Saudis have approached Pakistan for help in case they need it, meaning that they don't trust the Americans and the Israelis anymore.

RK: Exactly. Whereas the Emiratis are moving closer and closer to the Israelis.

TA: Indeed, they're getting very close to Israel, effectively behaving like a parasitic state, politically and militarily. And the Qataris now seem to have broken, though who knows. They've asked the American troops to leave Qatar, for the US base to be closed, and have publicly declared, "We may have differences with Iran, but we are siblings." And often there are sibling rivalries, they said, which we must try and transcend.

RK: The Qataris share a huge gas field with Iran. They cannot differ too much with Iran. In fact, neither country can afford to differ too much with the other, but in particular, the weaker, smaller one cannot afford to differ with the bigger, stronger one. So you're right, this has thrown the cat among the pigeons, among the Gulf countries, as it were. And their relationships with the United States, their positions with regard to Iran, to Pakistan, to other potential allies in the region—all these relationships are now totally unclear. Even the Saudis have been talking to the Pakistanis, the Turks, and the Egyptians for quite a while, presumably with the idea of creating some kind of structure that might support them and protect them, meaning that the American umbrella is full of holes—which we've seen, since Iranian missiles and drones went through it without any problem. I think this has knocked the chessboard onto the floor. Now they must start again, in all of these relationships. It's very hard to say where that's going to go, but without question certainties, or what were assumed to be certainties, no longer exist.

TA: Coming back again to the reaction in the United States, which is very hostile, as you pointed out, especially among younger people—but at the level of the DNC and the Democrat leadership, they're behaving like they've always done. No serious opposition to Trump at all. This is provoking the younger generation of voters to challenge AIPAC, attack Israel, and challenge many of the old, tired, stale collaborationist, pro-Zionist incumbents in primaries across the country. One shouldn't exaggerate the impact, but one must register that there is a counter-movement as well.

RK: Absolutely. An equally interesting transformation may be happening within the Democratic Party, including its mainstream. We spoke in January about the failure of the Democratic Party leadership to register the popular shift in support for Palestine. This is still overwhelmingly the case, but in April, forty of the forty-seven Democratic senators voted against sending armored bulldozers to Israel. Such a vote could never have happened even a few years ago. The war against Iran may push this even further. They understand that, led by Israel, Trump has taken the United States into very dangerous waters with the war in Iran. But the Democratic leadership, as you say, hasn't changed one iota.

TA: Despite the fact that all their populations are against the war in Iran by quite large majorities, including ordinary Germans who are not only opposed to this war against Iran, but also to the Gaza genocide, the European elites do nothing. They are aware of how unpopular their countries' support for these outrageous wars are, but apart from Spain, Ireland, Belgium, and Slovenia there has been little formal criticism of or resistance to US and Israeli aggression. Spain, in particular, has been incredibly sharp and fearless in some of its criticisms and demands on the EU to break with Israel. Some countries, like Italy, may be shifting, it seems, because of pressure from below. Three general strikes, dock workers refusing to load ships bound for Israel, have made Meloni scared. She doesn't want to lose the election in 2027. But here in Britain they're trying to ban demonstrations. All to prevent public criticism of Israel.

RK: It's appalling. You're going back to before 1688, before there was a declaration of rights—not just in Britain, but in both the United States and France, as well. The United States has a Bill of Rights, which is being trampled on in order to protect Israel, not so much by law as by administrative fiat. In France, on the other hand, they are actually about to pass a law, or at least they're trying to do so, which basically legislates against criticism of Israel by describing it as antisemitism. In the UK, of course, you have this ridiculous Palestine Action proscription under an intentionally ill-defined terrorism law. So you have countries with long (albeit imperfect) histories of democratic traditions grounded in some form of rights—in the case of France, the Declaration of the Rights of Man; in the case of the United States, the Bill of Rights; in the case of Britain, the Glorious Revolution and Magna Carta—whose elected politicians are tossing all of this out the window to protect Israel, and this when they know full well that a majority of their populations are opposed to the genocide and war. These politicians, who belong to parties from across the political spectrum, are totally committed to every lie about Israel that has ever been told. They baselessly repeat the fiction that whatever Israel does is in protection of its security. "They bomb Beirut and kill hundreds of civilians in self-defense." Excuse me? These people continue to mouth these words, even as public opinion recognizes and calls out their lies.

That reflects the European elites' pitiful, disgraceful unwillingness to separate themselves from the United States over Iran, or over Israel. I don't believe they actually support starving people in Gaza. I don't think they actually believe the massacre of 75,000 people, of whom almost 90 percent were civilians, was necessary for Israel's self-defense. And they certainly don't believe in the US–Israeli war on Iran, which could cost all of them their jobs very soon because gasoline and diesel prices are going to climb so high that every government will be threatened electorally. They don't even have a sense of self-preservation. They're that slavishly devoted to this relationship with the United States, whether over Israel or foolish wars in the Middle East.

TA: It's been very revealing at the cost of Palestinian lives, and Iranian and Lebanese lives now, how deep European leaders' slavish devotion, as you put it, to the

United States has remained since October 7. Some had thought, though I must say I wasn't one of them, that the whole decolonization process would have taught these populations, the new generations, how destructive and ineffective such attempts to violently crush independence movements always are. Clearly that lesson hasn't been learned by either Europe or the US.

RK: Germany, France, Britain have, I think, yet to come to terms with their colonial past. They've yet to come to terms with the fact that the people who are "problems"—the immigrant populations, in their minds—are there because of their own imperialism and colonialism. If you colonize the Caribbean and dislodge indigenous social and economic systems, imposing slavery, you will eventually have Caribbean populations who are compelled to go to the metropole to do the work that many of your own citizens won't do. None of these countries have come to terms with any of that, neither with their responsibility, nor with the fact that these are outcomes that are a result of what they did in their empires over a century and a half or two, or over nearly four centuries, in the case of the Caribbean.

TA: Today, there is an opposition on the streets and elsewhere, so people do feel a sense of responsibility for what their countries are allowing to happen in Palestine. And a majority of people are against it. But even as the deaths continue, people are sleepwalking to their workplaces every single day. They know what their governments are doing. They know how they're behaving. It has an impact on them, but they feel helpless because their governments have ignored and repressed every effort to compel them to put a stop to it. If one opposes Israel's genocide of the Palestinians they are accused of antisemitism, terrorism, and so on. Germany is an obvious case, but France has been among the worst in imposing intense censorship on its population. This is particularly visible when one takes account what can and what cannot be published. It's changing a bit now . . .

RK: It's only beginning to change in France. I have been very impressed by the degree to which the book publishing industry in many countries, the United States and the UK, Spain and Italy, for example, are open to the publication of books that would never, under any circumstances, have been published ten years ago. And it's one of the few cultural spheres where the hegemony of censorship of any criticism of Israel has collapsed or has broken down. Major publishing houses would not publish books of a certain nature ten years ago and are now competing with one another to publish books on Gaza, to publish Palestinian poetry, whatever it may be. In all of these countries, I understand, but France is the last. The example of my own book *The Hundred Years' War on Palestine*, published in 2020, is an interesting anecdotal case. I have Slovenian translations, Basque translations, Korean and Vietnamese translations. Literally dozens of translations. The book was finally published in French in January 2026, but after how long? What did it take to reach the point where a French publisher was willing to put it in print?

TA: The speed with which the entire literary, cultural, political establishment in France bows to the dictates of what is required of them is astonishing. This pattern has been going on in France really since the late 1970s and has only intensified since the onset of the genocide. I think about it sometimes psychologically, and I wonder if they are trying to make up for the fact that the bulk of the country accepted the German occupation during the Second World War?

RK: I was about to say the same thing, Tariq. I think you're completely right.

TA: This is their penance, saying, "Oh, we made a huge mistake." France started deporting people to the camps before the Germans asked the Vichy government to do so.

RK: In France, the Gestapo did not directly deport a single person, neither French nor foreign Jews, to the camps. It was the French, the Vichy government, that handed them over to the Nazis to put them on the trains. So there's a deep sense of culpability and guilt, justifiably, which has been, I hate to say this, weaponized in defense of Israel. It's very similar to the situation, I think, in Germany. The death camps were not in France, of course, but the deportees to the death camps were handed over by the French government. And I don't think France has come to terms with that. They bought into the Gaullist myth that everybody resisted, which they didn't.

TA: "Everyone was in the Resistance." It's a total joke. Some years ago, I was investigating the composition of the Resistance for a talk I was going to give, and I was quite taken aback to find that the majority of those who were in the French Resistance, the majority, were not ethnic French. They were Spanish refugees from the republic, Italian Communists, Armenians, Algerians, all kinds of foreigners.

RK: Absolutely. That's of a piece with the liberation of the south of France. Following the Allies' success in Normandy, they invaded the south in a landing operation called "Operation Dragoon." The Free French Army was made up of one white armored division and several Moroccan, Senegalese, and Algerian divisions. The two divisions that liberated Marseille, at the cost of 5,000 soldiers killed, were from a Moroccan division and an Algerian division.

In all of these cases—and the same dynamics apply to Britain, as well—we're talking about the aftereffects of colonialism and the aftereffects of the Second World War and the Holocaust, which I don't think any of these countries has really fully come to terms with. All of this, as I said, is in a certain sense being weaponized to maintain a status quo, which I don't think serves the peoples of any of those countries.

TA: We've discussed many times now the vacancy of the misnamed Palestinian Authority, which has done nothing to obstruct Israel's genocide in Gaza. There's no one in the PA now who can even masquerade as a popular leader. Marwan Barghouti, perhaps, but he's been in prison for the past twenty-five years and the Israelis have no intention of letting him out.

RK: Exactly. That's the point. There's nobody free or inside Palestine who could play any kind of unifying political role. And that's why they will keep Barghouti forever and others like him, who understand that you have to unify the Palestinian national movement on a new basis. That terrifies the Israelis. And also, I would argue, the Americans. I don't think it's just the Israelis—it's a collective understanding that you cannot let the Palestinians have democratic self-representation because they will use it as an opportunity to start to act against American and Israeli interests. Whereas this format of a Palestinian Authority does exactly as it's told, rather than what has to be done: the public diplomacy and the development of a strategy for the unification of the Palestinian national movement. The Americans and the Israelis know that the Palestinian Authority will never do that.

TA: How do you explain Hamas's failure to develop such a strategy, given that they haven't been totally defeated?

RK: This is one of my great critiques of people who talk about armed struggle and resistance. Armed struggle and resistance are the right of any occupied, colonized people as a general principle. However, if you look at any successful national liberation movement, they weren't just doing that. In 1918, the Irish republican party Sinn Féin won a landslide victory in British parliamentary elections. Every one of Sinn Féin's elected members of parliament then withdrew from Westminster, went to Ireland, and said, "We are the parliament of the people of Ireland, the Dáil, and we proclaim our republic." This was the most intelligent possible form of resistance. It wasn't just Michael Collins assassinating British intelligence officers, or the boys in Cork, West Cork, ambushing Black and Tan patrols. They were raising money in the United States, and they were doing propaganda in Britain, and they were doing fifteen other things which were unarmed resistance, alongside ambushing the patrols and assassinating British intelligence officers. The FLN did the same kind of thing. That's what Hamas doesn't seem to understand. The other thing is a very bitter truth: There is no colonial occupation without collaboration. Britain ran Ireland with the Royal Irish Constabulary. They had a huge military garrison, and whenever there was trouble, the British soldiers came out. But day in, day out, it was Irish people, many of them Anglo-Irish, many of them Protestant, but the bulk of the rank and file were ordinary Irish people. The Israelis are now creating militias in the Gaza Strip as supplements to their authority and control of the area, and that's what the Palestinian Authority is in essence. It's a standard colonial tactic.

TA: This is all true. But I think it's worth registering that the Zionist occupation of Palestine, backed by the British and later the US, is of a sui-generis type. Negotiating with the Israelis, as both the PLO and Hamas have discovered, is negotiating with a power that has absolutely no intention to leave of its own accord. So a settlement on the usual colonial basis is virtually excluded, since there is no metropole for the Zionists to retreat to. Algeria and Ireland are, of course, useful comparisons, but a closer parallel to the situation in Palestine/Israel is South Africa. South Africa was different in one key regard: The overwhelming size of the Black population made a negotiated settlement the only alternative, and once the Soviet Union had collapsed and the US understood that an ANC-run state couldn't be pro-Soviet, they gave up on the whites and pushed through the negotiated settlement in which the whites remained part of the country. Can this be done in Israel?

The only way there could be a single state with equal rights for all would be if the backers of Israel, which have kept the country going for seventy years, decided to stop backing Israel blindly. In existing conditions, what other option do the Palestinians have but to fight? Resistance, as you know better than me, always requires a diversity of tactics with the goal of negotiating a freedom settlement. Regardless of all the horrors, one objective fact cannot be denied: This latest phase of Israel's war on Palestine has alerted the entire world to the scale of Israeli oppression, and the ideological justifications used for the genocide that have pushed the International Criminal Court into declaring Netanyahu and three other members of his cabinet as wanted for war crimes. This entire war has shown the world that international laws and institutions are pretty much useless if the United States doesn't approve of what they do.

These revelations and realizations will undoubtedly help the Palestinians and those defending their right to resist. One of the problems has been, as we know too well, that Israel is opposed to all forms of criticism and opposition, not simply of violence. One obvious example is the BDS movement, which was an attempt to wage a nonviolent struggle in defense of Palestinian rights and whose successes have been quite remarkable. This movement, too, was viciously attacked by the Israelis, and its allied countries have been trying hard to make it illegal in their own spheres. The message sent by the Israelis and their allies is fairly straightforward: We are going to crush you, take all your lands and property, treat you as second-class citizens, but if you decide to fight any of this, you are terrorists and will be destroyed. That is the reality that faces us.

RK: It's true that Israel refuses to tolerate dissent. On top of that, you have elites whose interests are linked to the occupier quite frequently. Ghassan Kanafani did a brilliant class analysis of the failure of the 1936–39 revolt in Palestine in which he ascribes that failure, in part, to these class differences and the fact that the political leadership was drawn from a class which had shared interests with the British.[1] This doesn't necessarily mean they were collaborators, but they were incapable of taking the radical steps that might have changed things. Perhaps it wouldn't have—we don't know. I'm arguing, however, that those shared interests with the occupying power limited elite Palestinians' ability to mobilize the people and to oppose the British at an early enough stage. Ultimately, it was a mass uprising from below that forced them in 1936 to unify and to take a more nationalist, more radical political position. So, this is another element one has to take into account.

When I was in Palestine last December, I was shocked by the prosperity of Ramallah. Three glittering malls opened in Ramallah during the period of the genocide. It's like a little golden bubble. There are fancy coffee shops, there are expensive restaurants, there are upscale clothing shops. One can live a semi-ordinary life. The Israeli Army will come in and arrest people all the time, but they're much, much more shielded from that day-to-day colonial violence than anywhere else in the West Bank or certainly anywhere in Gaza. It's a really shocking sight to see. In a situation of genocide in particular, in a situation of occupation, it would be a terrible anomaly. This is worse. I was told that three malls had opened. I saw two of them, but I didn't go in them.

TA: I remember that I once met Mourid Barghouti, the poet, in Cairo, at his place. His wife was there, myself, and one or two other Palestinian comrades. He had just returned from Ramallah, and he said to me that the thing that shocked him the most was meeting people who were comrades of his in the past, in the PLO, in the political resistance, who were building these huge ugly houses in Ramallah. And when he asked them if this was necessary, they replied, "We fought a long time, let us have some fun now." I found this attitude rather shocking and often wonder why Palestinians in the West Bank don't revolt against the PA. I guess one reason why there has not been even a semi-uprising against the PA is because they have a lot of money and they pay for education and healthcare, which the Europeans and others supply.

RK: That is one of the major, if not *the* most important reason. You're absolutely right. Also, a lot of people understand that Israel is capable of unlimited violence. They know that revolting against the Palestinian Authority could unleash untold horrors, as we've seen in Gaza.

TA: Yeah, they could be wiped out.

RK: Young people who say, "I have no future, I have nothing to look forward to, I have nothing to lose," are in many cases willing to carry out acts of violence, often without organization and without any kind of planning or strategy, which by themselves are going to have little effect, and which in many cases cost them their lives or land them in jail forever. But most ordinary people say on the one hand, life is terrible, but on the other hand, they'll destroy my house if we rebel and they end up deciding, "I don't want my house destroyed." And I mean, one can't fault people who have families and so on for making that choice. On the other hand, you do have people who continue to resist in all kinds of different ways. Unfortunately, they do so without the kind of central organization and strategic planning that would be necessary for this to have any kind of political effect. Without, you can call it public diplomacy, you can call it propaganda, without a central unified strategy, none of this can amount to anything. That's the thing I'm trying to understand. What were the leaders of Hamas thinking, those who launched this operation starting on October 7, 2023? What was their strategic objective? And how did they think they would reach it? Now, it may be that they wanted to bring the whole region into chaos, in which case they've succeeded. Brilliant. But will that lead to the liberation of Palestine? Again, that's an open question. I was recently asked this question about October 7's strategic objectives in one of the talks I gave in France and I said, "Yahya Sinwar is dead, Mohammed Sinwar is dead, Ismail Haniyeh is dead, Mohammed Deif is dead. Every single person we know who might have had anything to do with the planning of Tufan al-Aqsa is dead. They've all been assassinated. So we won't know. We can only guess."

TA: These mass assassinations, wiping out whole indigenous political layers, is something which of course the Americans and the Brits have done for a long time in their colonies, but the Israelis do it with a particular unashamed vengeance.

RK: That's exactly what I'm working on right now: the way in which British counterinsurgency was developed into a doctrine at the turn of the twentieth century, used in Ireland during the war of independence and Palestine in the Great Revolt of 1936–39, and then passed on to the Israelis. Tens of thousands of Haganah militiamen were recruited first as auxiliaries to the British Army and the police, and many of them were trained by British officers like Orde Wingate in exactly these doctrines of attacking the civilian population. The notorious British officer Frank Kitson carried on this tradition and elaborated its tactics in a book published in 1960 called *Gangs and Counter-gangs*. Effectively, the colonizing country creates its own gangs to counter the so-called gangs of indigenous resistance. Assassination was a key British tactic in Ireland. This was not undisciplined soldiers or Black and Tans going off and burning Cork— It was approved by the Cabinet. Officers were taught to do this at Sandhurst, Woolwich, and the staff college at Camberley. A little over twenty years later, thirty-five Israeli generals came out of the Jewish Brigade of the British Army in the Second World War. Most of them had been recruited as auxiliaries to the British forces during the revolt and were trained by the British to deploy these tactics. Since then, they've improved upon what they'd been taught by their British mentors.

You notice that the Americans left to the Israelis, perhaps with American guidance and reconnaissance and so forth, the actual killing of the Supreme Leader Ali Khamenei. It was the Israelis who did it, as far as we know. There are also many other Iranian leaders who've been killed during this period—mainly, or perhaps entirely, by the Israelis. But given that the two collaborate so closely, this may be what we call in Arabic "the distribution of roles." One country does the reconnaissance, they decide on targets together, then the other country carries out the operation. I don't know. One day someone will tell us.

TA: What is well known is that after the Khomeini revolution in Iran in 1979, the United States effectively gave up on carrying out very intensive CIA operations in Iran and the Israelis took over. The US didn't give up on trying to overthrow the regime, of course.

RK: When people talk about the reasons that the United States clings to Israel, they usually point to the Israel lobby, sometimes to the utilization of the Bible to mobilize Christian evangelicals. As I mentioned in an earlier conversation, those are both very important. But I think it's these kinds of connections between the US and Israeli militaries, between their intelligence services, and between the US arms industry and Israel that are most crucial. The Israeli market for weapons and military technology is huge, especially for the most expensive and sophisticated weapons. And it would be a huge shock to the American military-industrial complex if Israel were not supported in purchasing these weapons by American tax dollars. This war with Iran has already cost $30 billion, including the cost of replacement aircraft engines that have worn out, planes that no longer can fly, and so on. That's the most important lobby: Raytheon, Boeing, and so forth.

TA: To return to Palestine, the major goal for the Israelis, of course, is to take it over, to completely occupy Gaza: "Eretz Israel." How close do you think we are to that, Rashid? The Israelis are carrying on behaving as they always do, not allowing food to reach Gaza, they're attacking flotilla after flotilla, and so on. The fact that the Iranians have resisted the Israeli–US aggression and bombed Tel Aviv and Haifa is encouraging. But Israel's publicly declared aim now is to take over the whole of Palestine, no mysteries, no secrets. Do you think they will succeed?

RK: When we had our last conversation in January, I had just returned from a trip to Palestine/Israel in December. I have to say that I came back with the sense that (a) you are right, they are trying to capture and empty Gaza and the West Bank of their population; and (b) they will never succeed. This is certainly not for lack of trying.

In the West Bank, and also in Gaza, the Israelis are attempting to squeeze the Palestinians into a smaller and smaller space, with the hope that they can eventually get rid of them by forcing them into conditions that are so unsustainable that they will be forced to leave sooner or later. This is a strategy the Israelis have been pursuing for some time. A couple of years before Bezalel Smotrich became Israel's minister of finance and a junior minister in the Ministry of Defense in charge of running the West Bank, he had already developed a plan to reduce the number of Palestinians and the amount of Palestinian land. That's what they're doing with the destruction of refugee camps in the northern part of the West Bank, as well as the devastation of dozens of West Bank villages by the so-called settlers.

We've seen the same playbook in the case of Gaza. The Israelis actually intended to drive people into Sinai with the support of the United States government after October 7. In October 2023, within weeks of the beginning of Israel's war on Gaza, the White House's Office of Management and Budget issued a supplementary budget requesting funds for Palestinians' removal from Gaza.[2] This request included money for Palestinians outside of Gaza. That same month, the Biden administration sent their little errand boy, then Secretary of State Antony Blinken, to Cairo, Amman, and Riyadh, to inform the Egyptian, Jordanian, and Saudi governments that the Israelis were going to kick the Palestinians out of Gaza. Blinken had been instructed to offer Egypt billions of dollars of debt forgiveness in exchange for accepting the mass exile of Palestinians from Gaza.[3] I understand that it was only under popular pressure, and a blunt warning from the Egyptian Army, that President El-Sisi refused that deal.

As we know, Israel hasn't relented on its objective of ethnically cleansing both Gaza and the West Bank of Palestinians. Still, it's not going to work. It's very hard to drive around the West Bank these days because they've erected hundreds and hundreds of new gates and arbitrarily close them. They don't even need to man these positions anymore. They used to have checkpoints with soldiers in body armor and snipers up above. Now, in addition, they have security cameras and operate the gates remotely. If you try to get out when the gate is closed, a drone will come and get you. There are hundreds of these gates, which surround every village. Some days they close some of them, some days they close them all. Meanwhile, the Arab communities inside Israel are being ravaged by state-supported gangs of Arabs armed to the teeth who are engaged in blackmail and murder—the murder rate is hundreds a year of Arabs killed by Arabs. This is Israeli policy.

In Itamar Ben-Gvir's first year as minister of national security, the murder rate of Palestinian citizens of Israel more than doubled. Just two months into this year, 2026, forty-six Palestinians had already been murdered in Israel. These are not family disputes. These are the victims of large gangs armed to the teeth with weapons purchased or stolen or smuggled across the border. Most Palestinian citizens of Israel are not allowed to carry arms, with the exception of the Druze who are eligible for the draft, but this is still allowed to continue.

The Israeli police don't deal with Arab-on-Arab crime. In spite of all that, these Palestinian Israeli populations are thriving. I went to what used to be a small village in the north and is now a small city. I asked a relative up there, "How do you manage in these conditions?" He said, "We pay them 500 shekels a week and we just charge our customers a little more and we're fine." So in my view, none of these measures, whether the gates, whether allowing the spread of gang violence, or the actual genocide, whatever it may be, are working. Maybe I'm over-optimistic, maybe I saw the wrong people in December, but my very strong impression is that you're right about what they're trying to do, but I'm suggesting that, and I hope that, they won't succeed.

Even these awful conditions are not going to force people to leave. When I talk to people in the West Bank, they tell me, "Nobody's going to make us leave. No way." The Arab population inside Palestine, from the river to the sea, is larger than the Jewish population. After a century of ethnic cleansing, they still haven't succeeded. I don't think they will.

TA: On that note, Rashid, I had better let you go and have your lunch.

Notes

1. May 10, 2024

1 Ghassan Kanafani, *The Revolution of 1936–1939 in Palestine: Background, Details, and Analysis*, New York: 1804 Books, 2023 [1972].

2 Kanafani, *The Revolution of 1936–1939 in Palestine*, p. 60.

3 Nasser's "Memoirs of the First Palestine War," translated into English by Walid Khalidi for the *Journal of Palestine Studies* 2, no. 2 (Winter 1973), is a riveting account of the chaos and deliberate lack of plan by the corrupted high command in Cairo.

4 Walid Khalidi passed away on March 8, 2026, in his 101st year.

5 Albert Hourani, "Ottoman Reform and the Politics of the Notables," in William Polk and Richard Chambers, eds., *Beginnings of Modernization in the Middle East: The Nineteenth Century*, Chicago: University of Chicago Press, 1968, pp. 41–68.

6 Popular Front for the Liberation of Palestine, a revolutionary socialist organization formed by George Habash and others after the 1967 War.

7 Seth Anziska, *Preventing Palestine: A Political History from Camp David to Oslo*, Princeton, NJ: Princeton University Press, 2018.

8 Shaul Mishal and Avraham Sela, *The Palestinian Hamas: Vision, Violence, and Coexistence*, New York: Columbia University Press, 2000.
9 Perry Anderson, "The House of Zion," *New Left Review* 96 (November/December 2015): 5–37.
10 John Mearsheimer and Stephen Walt, *The Israel Lobby and US Foreign Policy*, New York: Farrar, Straus and Giroux, 2007; the book expands on the arguments presented in "The Israel Lobby," *London Review of Books*, March 23, 2006.
11 Isaac Deutscher, "On the Israeli–Arab War," *New Left Review* I/44 (July/Aug 1967): 38–9.

2. January 9, 2026

1 "Trump Lays Out a Vision of Power Restrained Only by 'My Own Morality,' " *New York Times,* January 8, 2026.
2 "Which Countries Trade the Most with Israel and What Do They Buy and Sell?," Al Jazeera, May 22, 2025.
3 This assessment proved to be seriously mistaken during the American–Israeli war on Iran after this interview took place.
4 Since then, Trump has publicly admitted that the US poured in money and weapons to help their people in Iran, and he even complained that the Kurds had stolen quite a lot of these weapons.

3. May 1, 2026

1 Ghassan Kanafani, *The Revolution of 1936–1939 in Palestine: Background, Details, and Analysis*, New York: 1804 Books, 2023.
2 "Letter Regarding Critical National Security Funding Needs for FY 2024," October 20, 2023. Numerous news

outlets reported on human rights groups' concerns that these funds were intended to support the displacement of Palestinians. See, for example, "Biden's Israel Funding Request Gets Scrutiny, Hits Early Hurdle," Al Jazeera, November 1, 2023.

3 Edmund Bower, "Egypt 'Considers Deal to Accept 100,000 Displaced Palestinians in Exchange for US Debt Relief,' " *Telegraph*, October 15, 2023; Abdel Latif Wahba and Tarek El-Tablawy, "Egypt Denies Debt Relief Offered to Accept Gaza Palestinians," Bloomberg, November 16, 2023.